Warriors of The Old Testament

JOSHUA · KING DAVID · NEBUCHADNEZZAR · JUDAS MACCABEUS

MARK HEALY

Plates by RICHARD HOOK

BROCKHAMPTON PRESS

LONDON

First published in the UK 1989 by Firebird Books
P.O. Box 327, Poole, Dorset BH15 2RG

Copyright © 1989 Firebird Books Ltd
Text copyright © 1989 Mark Healy

This edition published 1998 by Brockhampton Press.
a member of Hodder Headline PLC Group

British Library Cataloguing in Publication Data

Healy, Mark
    Warriors of the Old Testament : Joshua, King
    David, Nebuchadnezzar, Judas Maccabeus.
    1. Bible. O.T. Characters
    I. Title
    221.9'22

ISBN 1 86019 4028

Series editor Stuart Booth
Designed by Kathryn S.A. Booth
Typeset by Inforum Typesetting, Portsmouth
Monochrome origination by Castle Graphics, Frome
Colour separation by Kingfisher Facsimile
Colour printed by Barwell Colour Print Ltd (Midsomer Norton)
Printed at Oriental Press, Dubai, U.A.E.

Contents

Joshua

CONQUEROR OF CANAAN

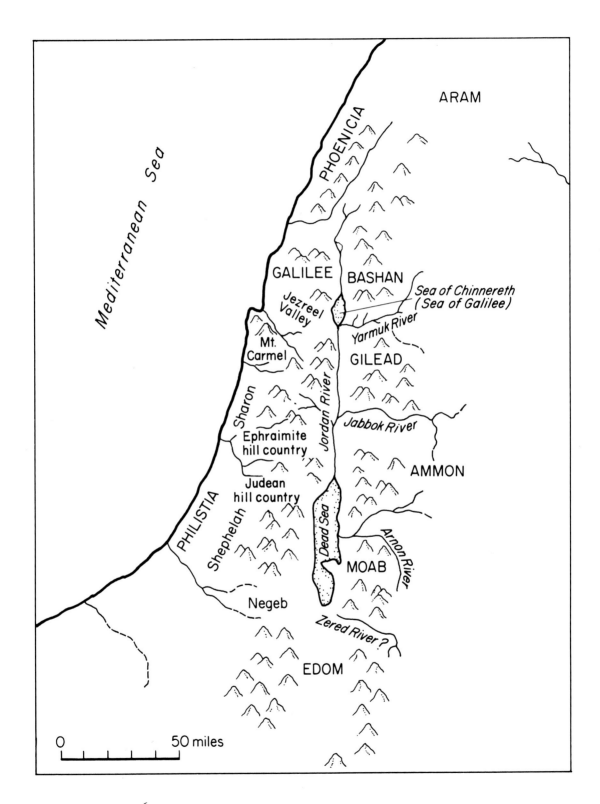

Joshua captured the entire country, just as Yahweh had told Moses, and he gave it as heritage to Israel to be shared out between the tribes.

(*Joshua* 11:23)

Warrior Son of Nun

On the face of it, the Bible tells a straightforward enough story of Joshua, the great Hebrew warrior and successor to Moses. He emerges in the *Book of Exodus* as the 'adjutant of Moses'; the first evidence we are given of his military prowess is when he is appointed by Moses to command an attack on the nomadic Amalekites, who were harrying the Israelites in what was probably a series of guerrilla attacks. Already the efficient commander, Joshua, 'defeated Amalek, putting their people to the sword' (*Exodus* 17:13).

Joshua continued in this subordinate role until Moses' death, when he took over the leadership of the Israelites. Moses had, not long before his death, nominated him as his successor:

Joshua, son of Nun, was filled with the spirit of wisdom, for Moses had laid his hands on him . . .

(*Deuteronomy* 34:9)

Under Joshua's command, the Israelites crossed the River Jordan and occupied Canaan, their Promised Land. Then he led them in the wars that followed their occupation of the land.

Moses had died without setting foot on the ground of the Promised Land towards which he had led his people; but he had welded the Israelites together during the long years in the wilderness and in a sense his work was done. What was needed at his death was not another charismatic prophet, not a second maker of a nation, but a practical soldier, a warrior. This was the part that Joshua played.

It seems to hang together well enough. But the man behind this story remains a curious and challenging mystery. Some scholars have doubted his very existence.

The problem lies in the sources upon which we have to rely. There is little or no corroborative evidence to be found in history or archaeology for the story as told in the *Book of Joshua* – and the purpose of that book was neither historical nor biographical but, primarily, religious. For its compiler, the most important purpose of the text was to show that it was through the action of God, not man, that Canaan was delivered into the

The likely appearance of the Amalekites and other tribes against whom first Joshua and later Gideon fought.

hands of the Israelites. After all, they were the chosen people of their god – Yahweh. Consequently, the concern of the compilers of the *Book of Joshua* was to describe the events through which God fulfilled his promise to give the Israelites a land of their own. This, naturally, means that Joshua has to be given a subsidiary rôle.

Joshua emerges as a leader who operates under the direction of Yahweh, upon whose word his actions are almost entirely dependent. On the one occasion, when he does not consult his God, but acts of his own accord by sending spies to assess the defences of the city of Ai, the enterprise ends in failure. So we never gain any insight into Joshua as an individual, because we are given none of the biographical information that might allow us to flesh him out as a person. It is only as the servant of Yahweh that he is presented, even at his death:

. . . Joshua, the son of Nun, servant of Yahweh, died; he was a hundred and ten years old. He was buried on the estate he received as his heritage, at Mount Timnath-Serah which lies in the highlands of Ephraim, north of Mount Gaash.

(Joshua 24:29–30)

Another problem is that the *Book of Joshua* was compiled hundreds of years later than the events it described, and was put together by editors who came from the southern kingdom of Judah. However, Joshua was a hero-figure in the traditions of the tribes of central Canaan, the forebears of the northern kingdom of Israel. The southern compilers probably deliberately 'edited out' Joshua because of the antipathy that had long existed between the tribes that formed the two kingdoms. Neither kingdom existed at the time of Joshua – both emerged from the much later political convulsion that split the united kingdom of Israel during the reign of Reheboam, successor of Solomon. So retrospective editing, the rewriting of history, has obscured our knowledge even more.

That being so, we have to approach Joshua in a rather roundabout way – to sneak up on him. We have to place his story, and those of the Judges,

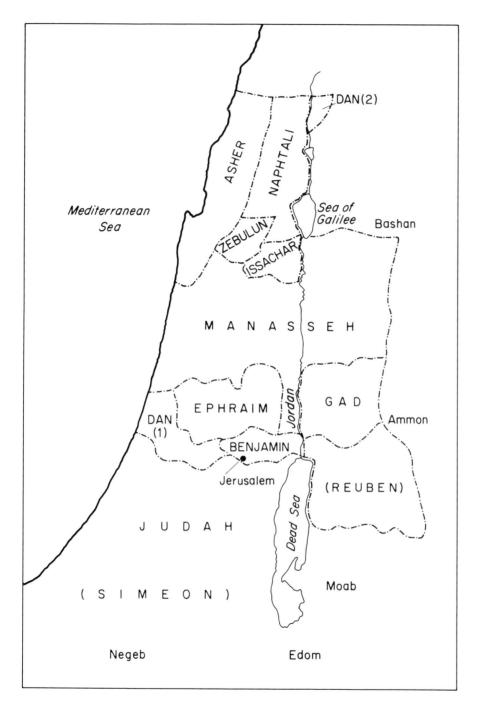

DAN(2)

ASHER

NAPHTALI

Mediterranean
Sea

Sea of
Galilee

Bashan

ZEBULUN

ISSACHAR

M A N A S S E H

EPHRAIM

Jordan

G A D

DAN
(1)

Ammon

BENJAMIN

Jerusalem

(R E U B E N)

J U D A H

Dead Sea

(S I M E O N)

Moab

Negeb

Edom

in a broader context. The conquest of Canaan must be seen as part of a much wider picture, embracing Canaan and its long relationship with Egypt. Furthermore, the story of the sojourn of the tribes in Egypt has to be set against Egypt's relations with infiltrating immigrants such as the 'Asiatics' and, in particular, the Hyksos. It was their substantial legacy

Division of the 'Promised Land' in territories awarded by Joshua to the twelve tribes. An idealised picture rather than one corresponding to actual events of the late twelfth century B.C.

that provided the impetus for Egypt's imperial drive in the New Kingdom period, creating a wider view of the world and utilising a military technology whose impact was to change fundamentally the basis of Egyptian power. Consequently, the introduction of the war chariot was to have a profound effect on the ability of the Israelites to deal with the warlords of the Canaan plains. It was the decline of Egyptian power in Canaan that created the conditions that allowed the Israelites to enter Canaan as intruders and successfully impose themselves on the land and in time take it for themselves.

This period is a rich tapestry of military, political and religious elements. All of them interact to form the immense backdrop to the conquest of the Land of Canaan by the Israelites.

Egypt and Exodus

Because, as we have seen, Joshua enters upon the stage of history as a military commander appointed by Moses, he is in a very real sense a child of the Exodus. He is a product of the most pivotal event in the long history of the Jewish people, when the Hebrews escaped from their bondage in Egypt and set out on their journey to the Promised Land. The story is recalled annually today by Jews the world over when, at the celebration of the Passover, the head of the household reads aloud the story of the Exodus.

The Despised Asiatic

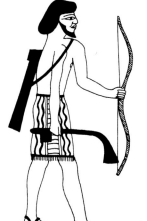

This Semitic nomad warrior, again based upon Beni-hasen painting, shows the duck-billed axe, double convex bow and quiver that were the standard weapons around 1900 B.C. and with which Joshua's men would have been armed.

The Exodus itself had its roots deep in the Hebrews' past, for they had been resident in the kingdom of Egypt for hundreds of years. They were among a number of tribes – known collectively to the Egyptians as 'Asiatics' – who from time immemorial had infiltrated Egypt from beyond its eastern borders, in particular from Canaan and Syria. The Egyptians looked upon them with contempt mixed with fear, 'the wretched Asiatic', strange peoples with strange ways. A document from the Tenth Dynasty (2134–2040 B.C.) says:

bad is the country where he lives, inconvenient in respect of water, impracticable because of many trees, its roads are bad on account of the mountains. He does not settle in one place, for [lack of] food makes his legs take flight. Since the day of Horus he has been at war, he does not conquer, nor yet can he be conquered.

Not surprisingly, the Asiatics found Egypt preferable to their own homelands and brought their flocks to graze in the Nile delta.

To Egyptian eyes, there would have been nothing to distinguish the Hebrews from any other Asiatics. They had come to escape famine in their own territories in Canaan and they settled – with their cattle, their sheep and all their other possessions – in the land of Goshen, the eastern district of the Nile delta.

The Hyksos

Egypt tolerated these nomad tribes because they brought some economic benefit to the country, but they were always difficult to contain. In the end, one more powerful and better-organised group, the *Hikau Khasut* or *Hyksos*, effectively took control of Egypt. Exploiting Egyptian political weakness, itself a consequence of a complex of factors, the Hyksos were firmly ensconced in the eastern delta as early as 1720 B.C. and were sufficiently strong to capture the old Egyptian capital city of Memphis in 1674 B.C. After that, Egypt was ruled by foreign (Hyksos) kings, for although the Hyksos rulers physically occupied only Lower Egypt, their power and influence was such that the rest of the country was reduced to a state of virtual vassaldom.

These Hyksos pharaohs, Egypt's Sixteenth Dynasty, so far from imposing an alien culture on Egypt adopted and borrowed extensively from the civilisation over which they ruled. Their names were written in hieroglyphs, they adopted Egyptian throne names and, in the manner of the Pharaohs, they instituted an official religion modelled on that of Egypt. They were so like the native rulers in maintaining a continuity with Egyptian culture and tradition that many in Egypt acquiesced quite contentedly with their rule.

House of Joseph

They retained, too, an essentially Egyptian bureaucracy, but they permitted other 'foreigners' to rise to positions of considerable power within it. The story of Joseph is thus credible in principle, even though it is presented in the Bible in a way whose detail suggests that much of it is fictitious and even though, again, it is recounted for theological rather than historical purposes. Joseph, the favourite of the many sons of the Hebrew patriarch Jacob, rose from being a household slave in Egypt to

Peaceful trade was tempered by the Egyptian policy of punitive campaigns in the Sinai and Canaan – and so the image of the Pharaoh 'smiting the Asiatic' became a recurring motif in Egyptian art.

become governor, or vizier, of the whole of Egypt. He took an Egyptian wife, by whom he had two sons, Manasseh and Ephraim, whose descendants became known as the House of Joseph.

At a time of widespread famine his father Jacob, in Canaan, sent his brothers to Egypt to buy grain. Joseph provided them with grain, and revealed his identity to them. Then he asked them to bring Jacob to be re-united with him in Egypt. So Jacob came to live 'in the best of the land; in the land of Goshen' and he and his descendants and all the Hebrews lived peaceably enough under the apparently tolerant rule of the Pharaohs.

We cannot with any confidence ascribe a date to the Joseph story. It would fit in with what we know of Egyptian history at any time from about 2000 B.C. to 900 B.C. The events described, though, drop most neatly into the Hyksos period – at no time afterwards did any Asiatics hold as much sway in Egypt. A career like Joseph's would have been far less credible at any other time.

Probably, however, the only near-certainty that emerges from this whole Joseph story is that a number of tribes from Canaan migrated to Egypt as a consequence of famine and that they remained in Egypt for a very long period of time.

Slavery

The Hyksos were finally expelled from Egyptian soil by Amosis I, the first pharaoh of the Eighteenth Dynasty. In a series of campaigns, Memphis was captured and the Hyksos capital, Avaris, in the delta, was sacked. With the tolerant Hyksos rulers gone, in about 1550 B.C., it is possible that life was not so easy for the descendants of Joseph in Egypt. Under the rulers of the Nineteenth Dynasty conditions worsened still more.

The substantial change in the Hebrews' circumstances, from those revealed in the Joseph narrative at the end of *Genesis* to the desperate state described at the beginning of *Exodus*, is explained in the Bible by the simple statement that 'There came to power in Egypt a new king who had never heard of Joseph', who introduced taskmasters over the Israelites to wear them down by forced labour.

Biblical scholars now tend to agree that the Pharoah identified here – the pharaoh of the Exodus – was Ramesses II, who ruled Egypt for the greater part of the thirteenth century B.C. Soon after his accession, he embarked upon the building of a new, fortified residence city, bearing his name, together with a smaller satellite 'store' city, Pithom, both in the eastern delta. This was the land in which the Hebrew tribes grazed their flocks. A vast labour force was needed to build these new cities and for the unskilled tasks – the heavy labouring, the brick making and the mortar mixing – the Hebrews were a convenient pool of manpower. The bondage they endured as forced labourers was harsh.

Even from an early period, it seems that the skills of the Semitic musicians were highly prized by the Egyptians, in whose employ they readily found work.

The Great Escape

How, led by Moses, the Hebrews fled from their slavery in Egypt into the desert of Sinai is told in the *Book of Exodus*, in what must be the greatest escape story of all time. Yet we have few hard facts to go on. The historical evidence is scanty, and the Bible story regards the Exodus as a divine deliverance rather than an epic.

It is generally accepted that the Exodus from Egypt took place during the long reign of Pharaoh Ramesses II. He is depicted here in the famous granite statue from Elephantine.

13

If we accept that the reference to Israel on the Merneptah Stela is to the House of Joseph that came out of Egypt under the leadership of Moses then it would be reasonable to date the Exodus around 1270–1260 B.C. However, such a date presupposes that the Hebrews really did spend 'forty years' in the wilderness, which may be doubtful given the significance of the figure forty to the Biblical writers. It is entirely possible that the wanderings in the Sinai occupied a much shorter space of time.

Of one matter, however, there seems to be little doubt. The number given in the Bible of the people who came out of Egypt is plainly exaggerated or in error:

The Israelites left Ramesses for Succoth, about six hundred thousand on the march – men, that is, not counting their families.

(*Exodus* 12:37)

This would mean a total of some two and a half million people – a figure that would give a column some 150 miles long of people marching ten abreast. It seems much more reasonable to accept the view that this passage from *Exodus* is quite late and that the figures represent the entire population of Israel at some later time.

It is not at all certain that all those who left Egypt travelled to Canaan as one group. There are a number of traditions preserved which imply that they did not. It seems, too, that, so far from 'all Israel' being involved in the sojourn and subsequent servitude in Egypt, only those related to the House of Joseph – that is the descendents of Manasseh and Ephraim – were involved. Many of the other tribes that came to form the later tribal

The Book of Exodus *tells of bricks made by the Israelites. They would have been of a type very similar to this one, bearing the royal stamp of Ramesses II.*

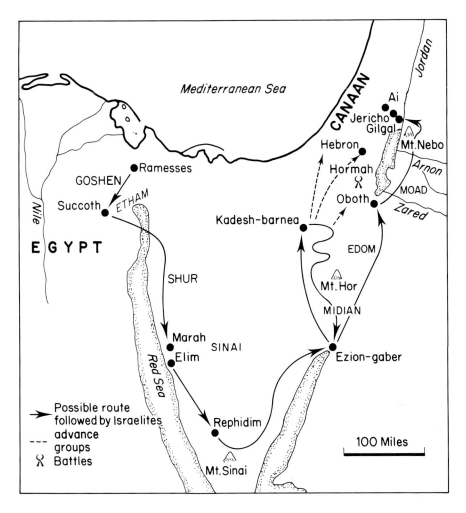

Traditional route of the Exodus from Egypt.

confederation were either already resident in Canaan and had been so for many hundreds of years, or they were not related to the Hebrews at all, being Canaanites who joined with the invaders under Joshua and entered into the covenant that ultimately bound the Hebrews together at a later date, possibly at Shechem.

We do not even know the route of the Exodus – indeed it is more likely that there was no single route, but that a number of different Hebrew groups left Egypt by different routes and made their own different ways across the Sinai peninsula.

Hyksos Military Legacy

The Hyksos bequeathed to the Egyptians much that was to be of great benefit. Under the Hyksos Pharaohs, Egypt became open to new

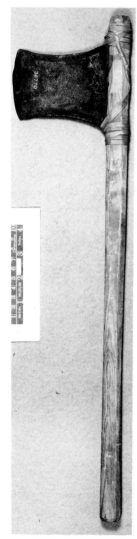

influences from Canaan and Mesopotamia and to new ideas in religion, art and philosophy. But it is in the military innovations that occurred in Egypt because of the Hyksos domination that we can see the greatest immediate impact. Out of the bitter lessons of nearly a century of warfare with the Hyksos, the Pharaohs of Egypt created a powerful and highly effective army with which they were to forge for Egypt an empire in Canaan and beyond.

The Hyksos were able to gain an initial foothold in Egypt because they effectively exploited the country's political weakness. But they gained and maintained their dominance because their military technology was more sophisticated than that of the Egyptians. The Hyksos had the chariot, the compound bow and bronze weaponry and these gave them an overwhelming superiority in battle. When finally, the native Theban pharaohs of the Eighteenth Dynasty were able to overthrow Hyksos power it was largely because they had by now acquired these weapons and learned to use them in a highly effective manner.

It is these weapons and tactics that were to dominate warfare in Egypt and beyond – and, especially, Canaan – for the next five hundred years.

The Chariot

The first chariots probably appeared in Mesopotamia, at least a thousand years before the Hyksos introduced them into Egypt. They had two or four solid wheels and were pulled by asses. The much more mobile spoke-wheeled chariot seems to have been introduced early in the second millennium B.C. in an area where the horse was known and already domesticated, perhaps northern Syria or northern Mesopotamia.

The chariot in the Bronze Age demonstrated a number of improvements. The axle moved further back to the rear of the cab, to provide a more stable firing platform for the archer and driver, although in Egypt it was not until the end of the fifteenth century B.C. that the axle was

The Book of Joshua *tells how Jericho succumbed to Israelite attack. On the seventh day of marching around the city, its walls collapsed. It was totally destroyed, together with its inhabitants.*

moved so far back as to be flush with the rear of the body. Egyptian chariots and their crews acquired armour. This has been illustrated on the walls of tombs – there is a painting of a bronze coat of mail from the tomb of one Kenamon, the steward of Amenophis II, and some relics of bronze scales were found in the palace of Amenophis III in Thebes.

For rapid transit, a rudimentary chariot design with open cab sides was employed, as is shown in this wall painting.

That the chariot had been introduced into Egypt by the Hyksos was acknowledged whenever in Egypt they were spoken of – the terms for the parts of the chariot were all borrowed from the Canaanite. Canaanites were used, too, both to drive and to maintain the chariots. Until the fourteenth century B.C. Egyptian chariots could not readily be distinguished from those used by the Canaanites, but during the reign of Tuthmosis IV the chariots begin to acquire a definite 'Egyptian' identity. Because they had became much heavier they were fitted with an eight-spoke wheel, although wartime experience saw the builders finally settle for six spokes. The chariot taken from the tomb of the young Tutankhamun, which dates from the second half of the fourteenth century, has a cab just over three feet wide and the width of the whole vehicle from wheel to wheel along the axle rod is nearly six feet. This, combined with a height of only four feet and a body width of just four-sevenths the length of the rod, suggests a vehicle both easy to control and, with a well-trained driver and horse team, highly manoeuverable – a vehicle at once agile and stable as a firing platform.

Horses

The Egyptians used two-man chariots. In this they had little choice, for

Caught in the mud, the 'iron' chariots of Sisera and the Canaanites succumbed to the attack of the Israelites swarming down from Mount Tabor under the command of Barak and Deborah.

they did not have horses large enough to pull heavier three-man chariots. The horses brought to Egypt by the Hyksos, and subsequently used by the Egyptians, would be described today as ponies, as is shown by an example found buried with full honours near the tomb of Senenmut, the chief steward of Queen Hatshepsut (1473–1458 B.C.). It is a small mare, standing not more than 12½ hands high.

It took some time for Egypt to become a horse-rearing country – climate and geography have not endowed the land with extensive acres of rolling grassland suitable for the grazing of large numbers of horses and horses were in short supply. Because of this, while the army of Amosis that finally ejected the Hyksos from Egypt did possess and use chariots we have to presume that the Egyptian chariot arm was at that time quite small, although no doubt swollen by captured Hyksos chariots. It remained relatively small until at least the time of Tuthmosis III. The maintenance of a chariot arm was always for this reason, a burden upon the state's resources. It became a major objective of its use in war to help acquire in the booty taken from the enemy other horses and chariots that could then be employed in the Egyptian ranks and used to swell the breeding stock in Egypt itself. Following the Battle of Megiddo, in 1458 B.C., some 2041 horses as well as 191 foals, some stallions and a number of colts were specifically picked out in the description of the booty taken from the defeated forces of the Canaanite alliance, some small indication of their importance to the Egyptians.

The Compound Bow
Although Egyptian soldiers of the Old and Middle Kingdoms had long employed the stave bow as their principal long-range weapon, it was through the Hyksos that they first encountered the much more formidable compound bow. The principal advantages of the compound bow lay in its greater range combined with a remarkable penetrative power. It is little wonder therefore that in many armies it became one of the standard weapons of war allowing combat to begin at quite long ranges. However, there is always a price to be paid for technological advance; in the case of the compound bow it was in the complexity of its manufacture. Additionally, its cost of production, arising principally out of the materials employed in its manufacture, meant it was not used by all the troops equipped as archers. Thus, in the Egyptian army of the New Kingdom it was common to find the stave bow employed alongside the compound bow, with the latter weapon being mainly restricted to the chariotry, who needed its penetrative power to deal with the armourclad crews of Egypt's enemies.

Some insight into the materials needed for production of the compound bow can be gauged from *The Tale of Aqhat*, an epic found on a number of tablets excavated at the site of ancient Ugarit in northern Syria, destroyed by the Sea Peoples in the twelfth century:

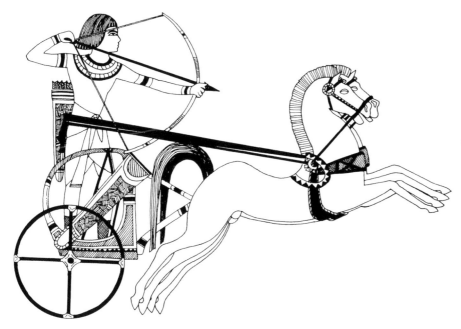

In this hunting scene from the early New Kingdom period (1430 B.C.), the Egyptian chariot reveals many of the features of the Hyksos design on which it is based. Characteristically, the single occupant has the reins wrapped around his waist to free the arms when firing the compound bow.

I vow yew trees of Lebanon,
I vow sinews from wild oxen;
I vow horns from mountain goats,
Tendons from the hocks of a bull;
I vow from arcane forest reeds:
Give [these] to Kothar wa-Khasis.
He'll make a bow for thee,
Darts for Yabamat-Liimmim

Thus, the process of creating a compound bow required materials from at least three animals and one tree. The arrows were made from reeds and fitted with bronze arrowheads (darts) which were necessary if the scale armour worn by the chariot crews of the enemy was to be penetrated. Thus, the equipping of an archer with a compound bow was a complex and expensive business.

The bows illustrated in Egyptian sources are either triangular or the recurved type. The materials from which they were constructed were very susceptible to warping due to changes in climatic conditions. Consequently, these bows were placed in their own cases when not in use and such cases can be observed on the sides of chariots. Some sense of the power of this weapon in the hands of an expert skilled in its use can be gauged from an account of the training of Pharaoh Amenophis II. He practised with the weapon from a chariot being driven at the gallop;

He [the king] entered into the northern garden and found that there had been set up for him four targets of Asiatic copper of one palm in their thickness, with twenty cubits between one post and its fellow . . . In his chariot, he grasped his bow and gripped four arrows at the same time . . . shooting at [the targets]. His arrows come out of the back thereof while he was attacking another post. It really was a deed which had never been done nor heard of by report: shooting at a target or copper an arrow which came out of it and dropped to the ground . . .

While other weapons made a significant contribution to warfare in the Bronze Age it was the chariot and the composite bow that were by far the dominating features of the battlefield. Their use released a level of mobility and destruction hitherto not seen in warfare. The Israelites, as we shall see, found the Canaanites of the cities of the plains formidable opponents because they were able to deploy weapons as destructive as these.

Conquest of Canaan

The most popular picture of the Israelite tribes coming into the inheritance promised to them by Yahweh is the Biblical account of the conquest of Canaan by the twelve tribes under the unified command of Joshua. The *Book of Joshua* gives a dramatic account of 'All Israel' participating in three campaigns in the middle, south and north of the country that see the destruction of many of the leading Canaanite cities and the subjugation of the people under Israelite rule.

The Promised Land

Bronze dagger from the thirteenth–fourteenth centuries B.C. Such a fine weapon would once have adorned the waistband of a high ranking soldier in the Pharaoh's army and inspired designs among the weapons of their enemies.

Nowadays, the name of Canaan is rarely encountered outside the pages of the Bible. Nevertheless, it was a term familiar not only to Joshua – and the people he led as the object of their predatory design – but also to many other ancient peoples. Evidence exists for the employment of the term in cuneiform, the diplomatic *lingua franca* of the ancient Near East. In that form, it occurs in texts from Syria, Phoenicia and Egypt. In the later period, the name was sufficiently understood by the Greeks and the Romans for them to employ it in historical writings. The geographical area to which the name refers is variously defined, but always centred on those lands identified with the more familiar (but much later) name of Palestine.

The origin of the name is still a matter of some dispute, although it is generally regarded as deriving from an Akkadian word *kinakhkhu*, meaning 'reddish purple'. As such, it would seem to have arisen from an identification of the land with the purple dye industry in ancient Phoenicia, which corresponds to the contemporary country of the Lebanon in addition to lands which now form part of Israel and Syria.

The first known use of the name is found on a magnesite statue of one Idri-mi of Alalakh, a city of some importance in the second millenium B.C. built astride one of the route junctions connecting northern Syria,

Mesopotamia and the Hittite kingdom in Anatolia. The statue dates from around 1550 B.C. when Idri-mi was ruler of Alalakh and a vassal of Parattarna, King of Mitanni. Idri-mi wrote his autobiography in a hundred and four lines of cuneiform inscribed all over the figure. He tells how he left his family in Emar:

I took with me my horse, my chariot and my groom, went away and crossed over the desert country and even entered into the region of the Sutian warriors. I stayed with them [once] over night in my . . . chariot, but the next day I moved on and went to the land of Canaan. I stayed in Ammia in the land of Canaan; in Ammia lived also natives of Haleb, of the country of Mukishkhi, of the country Ni' and also warriors from the country Ama'e. They discovered that I was the son of their overlord and gathered around me.

Idri-mi of Alalakh, on whose statue inscribed in cuneiform is the first known reference to the Land of Canaan.

There I grew up and stayed a long time. For seven years I lived among the Hapiru people.

Plainly the land of Canaan spoken of by Idri-mi lay to the south of his homeland and it would seem that the Egyptians understood Canaan to encompass the lands of modern Lebanon and Israel starting in the south at Gaza and stretching eastwards to the River Jordan and the Bekaa valley. Thus they applied it to a fairly limited geographical area, giving the name Retenu to the Sinai, Canaan and Syria combined.

Of all the Biblical allusions to the extent of Canaan one of the most detailed is that given in *Numbers 34* where the land as defined by Yahweh, the god of Israel, is more or less identical in its extent with the Egyptian province of Canaan at the end of the thirteenth century B.C. It seems that it was from Egyptian usage that the Israelites took over the term for the land that for nearly three thousand years has been bound to the history and destiny of the Jewish people.

Who were the inhabitants of Canaan at the time when Joshua led his troops into the land? We have already met the Hapiru, with whom

Dated from the same period as the el-Amarna tablet is this depiction of the captive Canaanite in chains.

One of many cuneiform tablets discovered at el-Amarna and dating from the fourteenth century B.C. in which Yapahu, the ruler of Gezer, corresponded with the Egyptian court as to conditions in Canaan. Mentioned in the letter are Hapiru, who are possibly identified with the Hebrews.

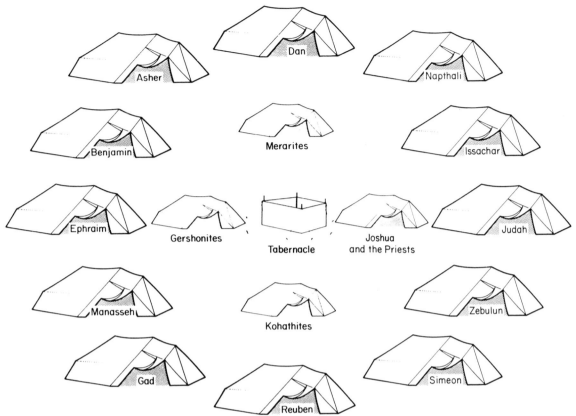

Idri-mi stayed. These seem to have been stateless freebooters who sold their services as mercenaries and, doubtless, as lawless bands, exploited any breakdown in the authority of the Egyptian overlords. The population was certainly a heterogeneous one. But mostly Canaan was comprised of small city states with a feudal social structure supporting an aristocracy of charioteers, known as the maryannu. Vassal responsibility meant that the king of each city state would in time of war call his maryannu to arms in the service of the pharaoh.

Invasion

Joshua entered Canaan, according to the Biblical text, at the head of some 40,000 warriors (*Joshua* 3:13) although at the battle of Ai he deploys only some 5000 (*Joshua* 8:12), which seems a more credible figure.

No information is given about the arms and equipment of the Israelite forces, but almost certainly their principal weapons were the same as those of other nomadic intruders into Canaan – the sword, spear and bow. Tomb paintings in Egypt show clearly that nomadic Asiatics were metalworkers and so it seems perfectly reasonable to assume that the Israelites were well able to make their own weapons. The main weapon would have probably been the bronze khopesh sword and the major

Like all desert tribes, the Israelites would have set up their camp with each tribe as a fighting unit in its specific position. But their encircled tents also protected the Tabernacle containing the Ark, which enshrined their covenant with Yahweh. This inclusion of all the tribes is in keeping with the Biblical description of 'all Israel' as the invading force entering Canaan.

long-range weapon the compound bow, whose method of construction was by this time widely known and whose assembly a task easily undertaken by nomads.

From Gilgal the tribes struck inland from the Jordan where some six miles north of the Dead Sea they came upon the city of Jericho.

The Battle of Jericho

Joshua marched the Israelites to within sight of the city walls at which the inhabitants, whom we know already from earlier on in the *Book of Joshua* to be panic-stricken at the coming of the intruders, shut the gates of the city.

Then, acting on Yahweh's instructions, for seven days, bearing the ark before them, the Israelites marched around the walls in silence, apart from trumpets sounded by the priests preceding the ark. On the seventh day, having marched around the city seven times, at Joshua's word of command:

The people raised the war cry, the trumpets sounded. When the people heard the sound of the trumpet, they raised a mighty war cry and the wall collapsed then and there. At once the people stormed the city, each man going straight forward; and they captured the city. They enforced the curse of destruction on everyone in the city: men and women, young and old, including the oxen, the sheep and the donkeys slaughtering all.

(*Joshua* 6:20–21)

But great difficulties are raised when this account is matched against archaeological evidence from extensive excavations carried out at the site. These suggest that at the time of Joshua's invasion Jericho was already a ruin; it had been destroyed in about 1560 B.C. While there is evidence to suggest that there may have been a small settlement at Jericho between 1400 and 1325 B.C., there is none to confirm that Jericho was a major city site in the time of Joshua. They are parallels elsewhere, though, for the stratagem that the Israelites are said to have employed at

24

Jericho. In a work on military ruses, the Roman writer Frontius reported:

When Domitius Calvinus was besieging Lueria, a town of the Ligurians protected not only by its location and siegeworks but also by the superiority of its defenders he instituted the practice of marching frequently around the walls with all his forces, and then marching back to camp. When the townspeople had been induced to believe that the Roman commander did this for the purpose of drill, and consequently took no precautions against his efforts, he transformed this practice of parading into a sudden attack, and gaining possession of the walls, forced the inhabitants to surrender.

(Yigal Yadin *The Art of Warfare in Biblical Lands*)

Destruction of Ai

Another military ruse was employed by Joshua in effecting the capture and destruction of the city of Ai. At dawn Joshua showed himself and a small force of five thousand men on the plain in front of the city. Thinking that they had an overwhelming superiority of numbers, the king and his forces came out of the city to give battle. Joshua pretended to retreat before them and so drew them away from the city. But the bulk of the Israelite force was concealed on the other side of the city, and this force occupied Ai and put it to fire. Seeing the smoke from the burning city, the people of Ai wavered and began to withdraw. Turning, Joshua and his men chased them back to the city, where the main Israelite force had deployed to act as an anvil to Joshua's hammer:

Although extensively excavated there is no archaeological evidence to support the otherwise widely renowned account of the destruction of Jericho described in the Book of Joshua. Nevertheless, it remains an intriguing and inspiring story of religiously inspired military achievement.

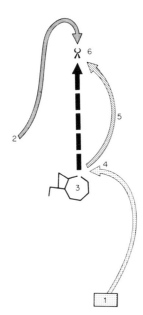

Joshua did not draw back the hand with which he had pointed the sabre until he had subjected all the inhabitants of Ai to the curse of Destruction.

(Joshua 8:26)

Once again, though, the biblical story is at variance with archaeological evidence. Excavations at Ai reveal that the site had long been a ruin when Joshua arrived at Canaan, having been devastated as early as 2000 B.C.

Southern Campaign

In the wake of the destruction of Ai, the inhabitants of Gibeon near Jerusalem entered into a treaty with the Israelites. This is explained away in the Bible as being a consequence of Gibeonite underhandedness, but it shows that the Israelite invaders were prepared to come to an accommodation with the natives where necessary. As a consequence, the King of Jerusalem, Adoni-Zedek, forged an alliance between himself and four other Canaanite kings, those of Hebron, Jarmuth, Lachish and Eglon. Combining their forces they advanced on Gibeon and placed it under siege. The Gibeonites sent word of their predicament to Joshua, who marched through the night and attacked the Canaanite forces at first light, pursuing the fleeing enemy down the defile at Beth-Horon. (Over a thousand years later Judas Maccabeus was to catch his enemies in the pass at Beth-Horon in a like manner.) The forces of the five kings were routed. The five kings were discovered hiding in a cave and taken to Joshua, who killed them and had their bodies thrown into a cave.

Joshua and the Israelites then moved south and conquered the cities of southern Canaan. It was a campaign of great destructiveness as the Bible makes plain:

Thus Joshua subjugated the whole country: the high lands, the Hegeb, the lowlands and watered foothills, and all their kings. He left not one survivor and put every living thing under the curse of destruction, as Yahweh, God of Israel, had commanded. Joshua conquered them as far as Kadesh-Barnea to Gaza and the whole region of Goshen as far as Gibeon. All these kings and their territory Joshua captured in a single campaign, because Yahweh, God of Israel fought for Israel.

(Joshua 10:40–42)

Again, though, we are in difficulties with the evidence. The cities described as being conquered by Joshua in this southern campaign were for the most part conquered by the Israelites only at a much later date. Jerusalem remained firmly in the hands of the Jebusites until it was taken by David some two centuries later. Indeed, we find in the *Book of Judges* (1:21) that the tribe of Benjamin who came to inhabit the area were unable to eject them from the city. Gezer is also said to have been taken by Joshua, but is known not to have been taken by the Israelites until the reign of Solomon. There would seem, in fact, to be no real evidence to support the picture given in the Bible of a southern campaign by Joshua and 'All Israel'.

The Battle of Ai. 1: Joshua's large force was hidden out of sight of the city's inhabitants, to the rear, awaiting his signal to advance. 2: Meanwhile, Joshua himself advanced towards Ai from Jericho with a hand-picked force of 5000, then feigned a retreat in the face of the advancing enemy. 3: Seeing the apparent retreat, the King of Ai ordered his forces out from the city to give chase, leaving it undefended. 4: At Joshua's signal, his hidden force attacked Ai, firing the city. 5: Seeing the flames, the army of Ai turned back, passing Joshua's force, who then attacked. 6: Simultaneously, the other arm of the Israelite force attacked from the other side. Ai and its inhabitants were totally destroyed.

Northern Campaign

The Biblical account has presented us thus far with an impression of an overwhelmingly successful military campaign carried out with ruthless despatch by Joshua and the Israelites. When the news of that success in the south reached the north of Canaan, Jabin, King of Hazor, determined to forge a coalition of Canaanite kings to oppose the Israelites. Hazor was one of the most important and powerful of the Canaanite city states and the coalition raised by Jabin was in theory the most powerful the Israelites had to face. The enemy forces were described (*Joshua* 11:4) as '. . . numerous as the sands of the sea, with a huge number of horses and chariots'.

The Canaanite forces chose to deploy their forces for battle at the site of the water supply of the city of Merom, whose king was present for the battle. They needed a plateau such as this to deploy and manoeuvre their chariots effectively.

The account of the battle at Merom is a little confused. The Israelite forces were able to negate the advantage of the Canaanite chariotry:

> Yahweh said to Joshua, 'Do not be afraid of them, for by this time tomorrow I shall hand them all over, cut to pieces, to Israel; you will hamstring their horses and burn their chariots.

> (*Joshua* 11:6)

Joshua and all the Israelites then fell upon the Canaanites until 'not one

Destruction of Ai, 'The Heap of Ruins', is attributed in the Bible to Joshua and 'all Israel'. Archaeology suggests that the site had been ruined for some centuries prior to the arrival of the Israelites in Canaan.

was left alive'. They hamstrung the enemy horses and burnt the chariots – although this would seem to have been a result, rather than the cause, of victory. Hazor was destroyed:

> [all the kings were] put to the sword in compliance with the curse of destruction, as Moses servant of Yahweh, had ordered. Yet of all these towns standing on their mounds, Israel burned none, apart from Hazor, burnt by Joshua
>
> *(Joshua 11:1)*

Once again it is difficult to assess the truth of this account. One problem is that Jabin, King of Hazor, is said to have been killed by Joshua yet is encountered again as king of a rebuilt Hazor in *Judges*, when we are told that he fought against and was destroyed by Deborah and Barak. Certainly Hazor was destroyed at about the time of Joshua's invasion of Canaan but it was a large city with strong defences and it is questionable whether it could have succumbed to the forces of the Israelites, who would seem to have found it impossible to take 'towns on mounds'. Their techniques in siege warfare were very limited at this stage and strongly built positions were too much for them. It may well have been, then, that Hazor was taken by the Sea Peoples, who were moving southwards at the time and had just destroyed the great cities of Alalakh and Ugarit.

Reality of Conquest

It is very difficult in the end to sustain the view propagated by the *Book of Joshua* that the land of Canaan was conquered by a mass invasion of 'All Israel' under Joshua. We are confronted with a picture of a remarkably successful invasion, masterminded by Joshua, who with three campaigns in the centre, the north and the south overwhelms the native Canaanite forces. The ultimate victory of the Israelite forces however is brought about because 'Yahweh, God of Israel, fought for Israel'. The vicious nature of this war against the Canaanites is not disguised.

The text is unambiguous about the consequences for the natives:

> All the spoils of the towns, including the livestock, the Israelites took as booty for themselves. But they put all the human beings to the sword until they had destroyed them completely: they did not leave a living soul. What Yahweh had ordered his servant Moses, Moses in turn had ordered Joshua, and Joshua carried it out, leaving nothing undone of what Yahweh had ordered Moses. In consequence, Joshua captured the entire country: the highlands, the whole Negeb and the whole of Goshen, the lowlands, the Arabah, the highlands and the lowlands of Israel.
>
> *(Joshua 11:14–16)*

The invasion of Canaan involved clashes with the Canaanites and in particular brought the Israelites into conflict with the Hupshu, the peasant soldiers of the city states.

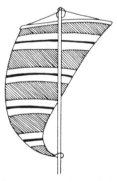

A common sight, frequently depicted in Egyptian paintings and reliefs, were the large sail-like standards, dyed in bright colours. They flew from the battlements of the Canaanite cities besieged and attacked by Joshua's forces.

However, a careful reading of the texts in *Joshua* and *Judges* reveals a much more complex story. The events described in *Joshua* 1–11 communicate the impression of a mass invasion directed towards the conquest of the whole of Canaan, but most occur only in the area later occupied by the tribe of Benjamin. When military operations do take place outside of this limited area it would seem that we are dealing with

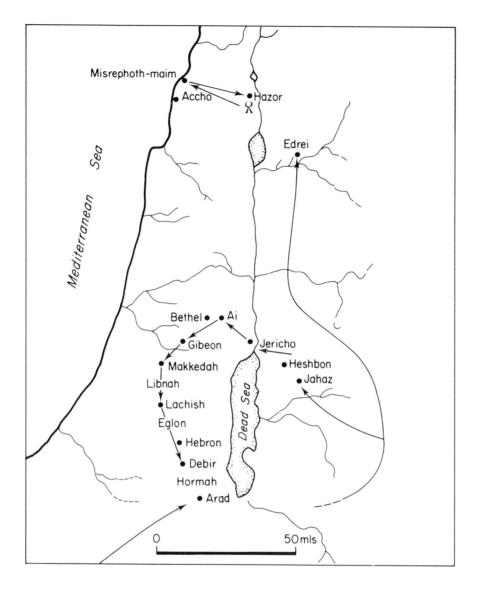

events that took place at a later date which have then either deliberately or as a consequence of confusion been attributed to the time of Joshua. However, even while that account is implying a 'total' conquest it is at the same time revealing that this was far from the case. The text has Yahweh speaking directly to Joshua towards the end of his life.

You are now old and advanced in years, yet there is still a great deal of territory left to be taken possession of . . .

(*Joshua* 13:1–2)

The conquests of Joshua, based upon the Biblical account.

The Archaeological Record
The graphic imagery of the destruction supposedly wrought by the forces of Joshua should in theory find ample testimony in the archaeo-

The later Canaanite chariots and their crews were better protected with bronze scale armour. Indeed, those encountered at Mount Gilboa were no doubt crewed by highly trained and well equipped maryannu.

It was the maryannu *or nobility, who, in return for 'fiefs' of land, gave service to the Canaanite kings of the cities as élite chariot troops.*

logical record of the period. However, this does not seem to be the case. Certainly the thirteenth century B.C., the period of the Israelite 'invasion,' was a time of widespread destruction of city sites in Canaan west of the River Jordan. Many people have seen in this evidence ample support for the historicity of the Joshua narrative, but there are many reasons for supposing that it was not the Israelites who were responsible for the destruction. In the first place, even where the destruction of sites can be securely dated to this period it is by no means certain that military action was responsible. Furthermore the primary sites whose destruction is described in some detail in the Joshua account of the conquest, such as Jericho and Ai, were not in the thirteenth century B.C. settled on anything like the scale suggested. Certainly, in the case of the 'city' of Ai, the evidence of excavation is that it was already a ruin when the Israelites arrived in Canaan, having been destroyed in about 2350 B.C. Paradoxically, where it is possible to demonstrate evidence of destruction of late Bronze Age Canaanite sites, they all involve cities that are not associated with the Joshua account.

A Different Story?

In the *Book of Judges* (1:27–36), which is regarded as being a more reliable and authentic account of the settlement than that found in *Joshua*, we find a different picture entirely. It is one of slow infiltration by various groups, with periodic eruptions of fighting between the incoming Israelite settlers. The employment of the phrase 'the Canaanites held their ground' gives us a good insight into the more likely conditions obtaining in Canaan following the 'invasion'. In reality, for the essentially nomadic Israelites entering Canaan, the natives with their superior military organisation and technology were tough nuts to crack. Never-

theless, as the Israelites in their turn became stronger they were able to take on the power of the native Canaanites.

The ultimate absorption of the Canaanite population was a process that itself took many hundreds of years. Thus, a more credible image is that of a limited invasion of the central hill country from east of the Jordan, under the leadership of Joshua, involving the tribes regarded as being of 'The House of Joseph'. Their actual military operations occurred in a small area. The success of these forces may have stimulated Hebrew tribes who had not entered Egypt but had always remained in Canaan to move against the Canaanites with whom they had been living for so long.

Thus, the process of settlement should be seen more in terms of a long-drawn-out process in which individual tribes addressed the situation found in their own areas. In some cases it is not inconceivable that they were supported in their moves against the overlords of the Canaanite cities by other disgruntled and economically alienated non-Israelite groups, who saw in the cause of the Israelites a solution to their own problems. While the evidence is not such as to allow any indisputable conclusion as to the exact nature of the settlement, it was plainly more complex than a cursory reading of the *Book of Joshua* would

Although the capture and destruction of Arad is part of the 'conquest tradition' it is now believed to have been conquered some centuries later. The two sites of the ancient settlement remain clearly visible.

31

Canaanite chariot from the thirteenth-fourteenth century B.C. showing to good effect the principal weapon in the arsenals of the kings of the city states. It was by burning such chariots and hamstringing the horses that Joshua was able to defeat the Canaanites of the north at the Battle of Merom.

suggest. The image of a mass invasion under divine guidance is not one that can be sustained even from the Bible itself. Far from being a mass invasion of 'all Israel' we find the various tribes acting in the early stages more or less independently. It is simply inappropriate to imagine one 'Israelite' nation acting in concert under one leader to realise a collective destiny to take the Promised Land by force of arms.

Judges

For many Biblical scholars, it is only in the *Book of Judges* that one encounters the first realistic picture of the political and social situation in Canaan in the period 1200–1050 B.C., the era before the emergence of the monarchy under Saul in about 1020 B.C.

This was a very turbulent period in Canaan, one in which the overriding political reality was the virtual disappearance of Egyptian authority. Indeed, following the defeat by Ramesses III of the 'Sea Peoples' on the borders of Egypt in about 1186 B.C., Egyptian authority in Canaan virtually ceased. The 'natives' were thereby allowed to attend to their own affairs without interference from the great southern power.

For the Israelite settlers in Canaan, the whole period was one of considerable upheaval marked by the absence of any centralised authority among the tribes. Indeed, the Judges seem to have dealt with problems or threats on the basis of individual or local tribal affiliation,

Striking swiftly during the 'middle watch', Gideon and his hand-picked force of three hundred destroyed the Midianites and the Amalekites, who for so long had been raiding settlements of their fellow tribesmen.

with any collective consciousness only appearing later. Significantly, this occurred towards the end of the age of the Judges and was brought about by the overall threat posed by the Philistines to all the tribes of Israel.

Thus, the *Book of Judges* is concerned principally with the conflicts between the Israelites and their Canaanite neighbours in a relatively small geographical area and with the Judges presented as saviours of their tribes or tribal groups.

The stories of the Judges' exploits preserve historical tradition but are structured in a theological manner, organised so that what emerges is called 'The Judges Cycle'. Religious editing of the exploits ensured that the Bible tells of a recurrent pattern in which the Israelites backslide from their commitment to the covenant with Yahweh, by worshipping Canaanite gods. Yahweh then sends oppressors to punish the Israelites, who then call on their God for mercy. Yahweh relents, and from amongst them 'chooses' an individual who is endowed with charisma 'to judge the people'.

Thus, the Judges were not in any way legal officials, but soldiers or local chieftains who saved their people as in the manner of the three we have chosen to concentrate on. Twelve are listed in the Bible, divided as major and minor characters. The exploits of three of the major Judges – Deborah, Gideon and Abimelech – provide a real insight into the conflicts between Israelite and Canaanite in the twelfth century B.C.

Deborah at Mount Tabor

At Mount Tabor, the ill-equipped Israelites, under the charismatic direction of a woman judge, Deborah, brought about the defeat through a clever strategem of a Canaanite chariot force, the very symbol of the military prowess of the city peoples of the plains. Deborah emerges from the account as a fiery leader of her people cast in the same mould as the ancient British Queen Boadicea of the Iceni. Through her inspired leadership a notable victory is realised over the only named Canaanite foe in the *Book of Judges*.

The Biblical account as it stands does – as we should by now have learned to expect – raise problems, not the least being that the enemy is the same Jabin, King of Hazor whose death is reported earlier in the *Book of Joshua*. It seems unlikely we are dealing with two separate kings of the same name, and reasonable therefore to assume that this is an error and to look for an alternative explanation.

We find that alternative source in 'The Song Of Deborah and Barak' in *Judges* 5, one of the oldest pieces of poetry in the Bible. It is a victory song commemorating the triumph of Yahweh over his enemies and praising

Laying siege to the city of Thebez, Abimilech was killed by the woman who threw a millstone at his head. Such an ignominious death was to become, in later times in Israel, a byword for military incompetence.

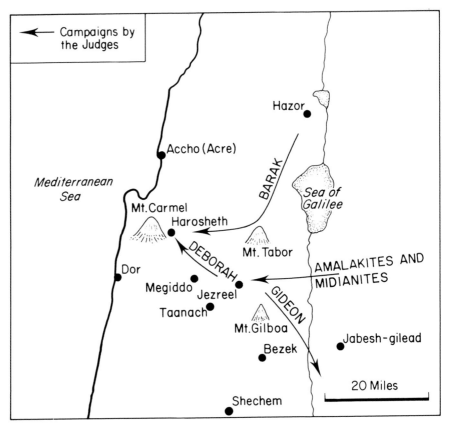

Campaigns by
the Judges

Hazor

Accho (Acre)

BARAK

Mediterranean
Sea

Sea of
Galilee

Mt. Carmel
Harosheth

DEBORAH

Mt. Tabor

AMALAKITES AND
MIDIANITES

Dor

Megiddo
Jezreel

GIDEON

Taanach

Mt. Gilboa

Jabesh-gilead

Bezek

20 Miles

Shechem

The campaigns of Gideon, Deborah and Abimilech.

the tribes – Machir, Benjamin, Ephraim and Issachar – who responded to the summons of Deborah to fight the foe. Composed (it is thought) shortly after the event, it describes how the Israelites defeated not Jabin but Sisera of Harosheth-ha-Goiim. Indeed, Jabin is not mentioned in the poem at all.

Deborah and Barak

Deborah was a prophetess who dispensed justice from under a palm tree in the hill country of Ephraim. Highly regarded for her wisdom many would come to her for a ruling in the case of disputes believing that in her judgements she was divining the will of Yahweh.

It is not clear why the Canaanites raised an army to attack the Israelites. It may have been as a consequence of Israelite pressure to break the power of the Canaanites, who were separating the northern tribes from those in central Palestine.

It is probable that the Canaanites had raised a large force. It is unrealistic, though, to accept at face value the claim (*Judges* 4:3) that they had 'nine hundred chariots of iron' – it would have been beyond the resources of any Canaanite city to deploy a chariot force of this size. In the fourteenth century B.C. the king of Byblos, a large and powerful city, asking for reinforcements from Egypt, requested only twenty to thirty

34

The rulers of the Canaanite city states regularly sent their tribute to the court of the Pharaoh whilst their land was under Egyptian domination.

Devastation of the great city of Hazor occurred at the end of the Bronze Age. Tradition has ascribed its destruction to Joshua, but it is just as possible that the Sea Peoples were responsible. Shown here are the remains of the Pillared Hall.

chariots, implying that this was as large a force as he could effectively employ. In the light of what is known of the small size of the Canaanite city armies, it would seem that even if we subtracted a nought and spoke of ninety chariots we might still be presuming too large a force. Nevertheless, ninety chariots supported by a large feudal levy would have comprised an army likely to have been perceived by the Israelites as huge and, given the fear engendered by the chariots, it is not surprising that the subsequent battle became one in which the defeat of the chariots was enshrined in the folk memory.

The chariots are described as 'of iron', which indicates that we are possibly dealing with 'Sea Peoples' rather than native Canaanites, for it is they who are credited with bringing iron working into Palestine. This would fit quite neatly with the speculation of some scholars that the name Sisera is not Canaanite and that Sisera may have been one of the 'Sea Peoples' who had established themselves on the coastal plain of the Palestinian Shepelah and then expanded into the Plain of Jezreel.

The Battle

The text is unambiguous about where the credit for the outcome of the battle lies. It is Deborah who had to cajole a seemingly reluctant Barak to take the field against Sisera. And the strategy, too, was Deborah's. It was based on an intimate knowledge of the terrain. Clearly the Israelites would stand no chance if they opposed the enemy on the plain, where their chariots could be used with devastating effect against the poorly equipped Israelite tribal levy armed only with spears, bows and swords. Somehow Sisera would have to be enticed on to ground where the power of his chariots could be negated.

Sisera was stationed with his army at Harosheth-ha-Goiim in the lee of Mount Carmel, but when he heard that Deborah and Barak had deployed their forces on Mount Tabor he decided to move, seeing in the Israelite disposition a threat to his line of communications with the north. As Deborah had foreseen, the Canaanite force advanced towards Tabor following the banks of the River Kishon. The Vale of Esdraelon

Canaanite charioteers in the time of Joshua and the Judges would have appeared little different from these based upon Egyptian paintings of the fourteenth century B.C. The warrior on the left carries his sword aloft, freeing his right hand to rein the chariot's horses.

Warriors of the 'House of Joseph' and of the later Judges, including Gideon and Deborah, were almost certainly very similar in appearance to these figures based on the Benihasen wall painting.

36

through which they advanced was a wide and fertile valley bounded to the north by the Hills of Galilee and to the south by Mount Gilboa and Mount Carmel. Along the southeastern edge of the vale flowed the River Kishon, normally a small stream flowing through an almost dry riverbed. However short, intense rainstorms transformed the river very quickly into a raging torrent and turned the deep rich soil of the vale into a glutinous morass inimicable to man, beast and chariot alike. Deborah's plan was dependent upon the elements playing their part and when the Canaanite army with the chariots in the van swung into view there must have been many anxious Israelite eyes looking skywards for the clouds that were to be the harbingers of their salvation and of the destruction of the Canaanites.

To the unsophisticated Israelites, the sight of Sisera's forces must have caused much fear and agitation and perhaps not a little silent questioning as to the wisdom of taking on such a formidable foe. As the sun glinted off the Canaanite shields and spearpoints and shimmered on the bronze scale armour of the charioteers doubt must have crept into the Israelites' hearts. Here below them, in all their martial glory, were the mighty chariots of the warlords of the plains. But as the sky darkened and the rain began to fall, the ground began to soften and the advancing chariots ground slowly to a halt as their wheels bogged down in the mud.

The 'Song of Deborah' paints a vivid picture of the Israelite soldiery pouring down the slopes of Mount Tabor and gaining a remarkable victory over the feared Canaanite chariots. As can be seen, the steep incline would produce considerable impetus in any descending forces.

This bronze arrowhead, from the period of the Judges is inscribed in Phoenician and dates from the eleventh century B.C.

The rain fell harder, turning the ground into a morass. Slithering and sliding horses, whipped relentlessly by their drivers, stumbled and fell. Above the sound of panicking men, the barked commands of the officers and the whinnying of the horses another noise could be heard – an immense roar as the rain on the mountain came pouring down into the riverbed, carrying all before it and overflowing the banks. As the Canaanites struggled to save themselves from the waters, Deborah turned to Barak, yelling with eyes ablaze:

Up! For today is the day when Yahweh has put Sisera into your power. Is Yahweh not marching at your head?

With only a slight hesitation and after one final scan of the mounting chaos in the valley below, Barak raised his sword and thrust it forward to signal the advance. Screaming a battlecry that could be heard even above the roar of the torrent, the crash of the thunder and the hammering of the rain, the Israelites scrambled down from the mountain and threw themselves into the wild mêlée of the now totally disorganised Canaanite troops. Jumping onto the chariots they dragged down the drivers and the mail-coated archers, their swords executing fearful carnage in the mud. Men and horses were ruthlessly despatched as the Israelites sought to exorcise with their blades the legacy of the hate and fear engendered over many years by the Canaanite chariots.

Song of Victory

Somehow Sisera was able to save himself from the slaughter, but as the 'Song of Barak' records with grim satisfaction he had not long to live. Some hours later, on foot and fleeing for his life, he came, exhausted and hungry, to a tent and presented himself to the woman within. The welcome he received gave no hint of the fate that awaited him:

> *Most blessed of women be Jael*
> *(the wife of Heber the Kenite);*
> *of tent dwelling women, may she be most blessed!*
>
> *He asked her for water; she gave him milk;*
> *she offered him curds in a lordly dish.*
> *She reached her hand out to seize the peg,*
> *her right hand to seize the workman's mallet.*
>
> *She hammered Sisera, she crushed his head,*
> *she pierced his temple and shattered it.*
> *Between her feet, he crumpled, he fell.*
> *Where he crumpled, there he fell, destroyed.*
>
> (*Judges* 5:25–27)

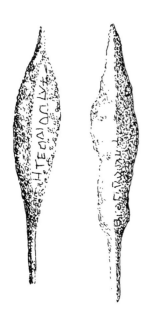

The significance of such inscribed arrowheads is that written Phoenician was the pregenitor of the Hebrew script.

The last few verses of 'The Song of Deborah and Barak' celebrate the great victory of Mount Tabor as a victory of the God of the Israelites over his enemies. The ultimate consequence of Yahweh's saving act in the battle against Sisera was that 'the country had peace for forty years'.

38

Gideon and the Midianites

The Israelites did what was evil in Yahweh's eyes, and for seven years Yahweh handed them over to Midian; and Midian bore down heavily on Israel.

(*Judges* 6:1–2)

Expressed in political rather than religious terms this means that the Midianites had established supremacy over the Israelites. That these nomadic raiders were able for so long to hold some of the Israelite tribes in thrall tells us much about conditions prevailing in Canaan at this time. The battle against Sisera had taken place in the western end of the Jezreel valley, but Gideon's exploits occurred in the eastern part of the valley. Clearly Egyptian influence and power in this part of Canaan had disappeared and the ease with which the nomadic Midianites were able to move into the area and terrorise and raid the Israelite settlements suggests that even the power of the Canaanite cities was in eclipse. It was also the lack of any central political authority amongst the Israelites that allowed the Midianites to inflict so much havoc on them and the distress they caused was great:

Whenever Israel sowed seed the Midianites would march up with Amalek and the sons of the east. They would march on Israel. They would pitch camp on their territory and destroy the produce of the country as far as Gaza. They left Israel nothing to live on, not a sheep or an ox or a donkey, for they came up as thick as locusts with their camels and their tents; they and their camels were innumerable, they invaded the country to pillage it.

(*Judges* 6:34–35)

The story of Gideon's defeat of the Midianites gives us a remarkable insight into the way in which the Israelites of the time fought a campaign and worked out their strategy. We can identify three distinct phases in the campaign. We have the recruitment of the forces, the preparation for battle and the planning of the campaign.

The Midianites and their allies, the Amalekites, encamped in the Jezreel valley with all their families, animals and other possessions. This provided Gideon with the opportunity he had been waiting for. Always before the Midianites had launched raids against the Israelite settlements in true nomadic fashion. They adopted hit and run tactics, utilising the speed of their camels to exploit the element of surprise and to extricate themselves from difficult situations. Because of this, the infantry forces of the Israelite tribal levy had been unable to come to grips with them. By bringing their whole settlement with them the Midianites had rendered themselves far more vulnerable to attack. It was their inability to move quickly, hampered as they were by the presence of their flocks and families, that Gideon intended to exploit. Having received the news that the enemy had encamped he sent word to call out the levy:

He sounded the horn and Abiezer rallied behind him. He sent messengers throughout

The Book of Judges *tells how the Israelites were seduced into worshipping Canaanite gods such as Baal. Consequently, Yahweh raised up enemies to oppress and punish them.*

39

Manasseh, and Manasseh too rallied behind him; he sent messengers to Asher, Zebulun and Naphtali, and they marched out to meet him.

(*Judges* 6:34–35)

The summons produced a force far larger than was needed by Gideon. His plan depended more on stealth and surprise than on fielding a large militia army. From the 32,000 men who responded to his call he selected 10,000 and from these he carefully chose just three hundred. His method of selecting these three hundred is deserving of some explanation, for on first reading it appears a strange way to select warriors:

So Gideon took the people down to the waterside, and Yahweh said to him, 'All those who lap the water with their tongues, as a dog laps, put on one side. And all those who kneel down to drink, put these on the other side. The number of those who lapped with their hands to their mouth was three hundred; all the rest of the people knelt to drink. Yahweh then said to Gideon, 'With the three hundred who lapped the water I shall rescue you and put Midian into your power. Let the people as a whole disperse to their homes.' So they took the people's provisions and their horns, and then Gideon sent all the Israelites back to their tents, keeping only the three hundred. The camp of Midian was below his in the valley.

(*Judges* 7:5–8)

Gideon may perhaps have chosen those who lay down to drink because they showed care to present the enemy with a reduced target as well as a willingness to tolerate the discomfort caused thereby. Such skill and hardiness was essential to his plan to destroy the enemy encampment.

Then he ordered the men of Naphtali, Asher and Manasseh to move against the water holes between the Midianites' encampment and the line of retreat that they would be forced to take in the aftermath of the attack. The task of these men would be to destroy the fleeing enemy in detail.

That night Gideon and his servant stole into the Midianite camp and overheard a conversation between two guards which revealed their low morale. After a final scout around the camp all was ready.

The Attack

Gideon had divided up his men into three groups of a hundred. He issued each man with a horn and an empty pitcher into which was placed a torch so that the light was concealed. Then he told them:

Watch me, and do as I do. When I reach the edge of the camp whatever I do, you must do also. I shall blow my horn, and so will all those who are with me; you too will then blow your horns all around the camp and shout, 'For Yahweh and for Gideon!'

(*Judges* 7:17–18)

Assigning each group to one side of the encampment – north, west and south – but leaving the east open so that the Midianites could escape towards the Jordan, Gideon ordered his forces down into the valley. As surprise was of the essence he took care to arrive at the edge of the Midianite camp at the dead of night. It was at the time of the middle watch, just after the guards had been changed; the new guards were not yet fully awake and their eyes were still unaccustomed to the darkness. Gideon stood up and his signal shout shattered the silence of the night: 'the sword for Yahweh and for Gideon!'

As if with one voice, his men took up the battle cry. Gideon took his clay pitcher, smashed it with his blade, and threw it at the nearest tent. He cut down the surprised guard. His men followed his example and poured into the camp. Flames leapt up as torches caught the tents alight. Panic-stricken Midianites scrambled into the night, stumbling and falling, their minds clouded by sleep. Babies cried and screamed as they clung to their mothers' breasts. The Israelites pushed into the camp, scything down the Midianites and shooting them with arrows as they emerged from their tents. They spared neither man, woman nor child. Amid the confusion Midianite killed Midianite in the half-light of the dancing flames. Gideon's men began to herd the enemy towards the eastern end of the camp. Acrid smoke from the burning tents drifted across the camp, and in the terror that developed many Midianites were crushed to death as they tried to escape the blades of the Israelites. Others disappeared, trampled beneath the feet of the snorting and grunting camels as, maddened by the heat, they blundered hither and thither. With their bronze khopeshes and iron swords, the three hundred slashed their way forward, inexorably pressing the surviving Midianites eastwards and out of the camp. The dead and dying were left behind amid a conflagration that was becoming one great funeral pyre.

With the survivors of the Midianite encampment in full flight in the direction of the Jordan, Gideon set off in hot pursuit, his intention being to finish the Midianite threat once and for all. After crossing the Jordan he finally ran to ground the Midianite kings, Zebah and Zalmunna, and killed them.

The men of Succoth, we are told, were unwilling to help Gideon and his men in their pursuit of the enemy. This suggests that they were not at that stage prepared to risk the vengeance of the Midianites should Gideon fail. Indeed, they demanded evidence that the Midianite kings were dead before they would give supplies to the Israelites:

Are the hands of Zebah and Zalmunna already in your grasp that we should give bread to your army?

(*Judges* 8:6)

The request was literally to be shown the hands of the dead kings. The presentation of some part of the body as evidence of death was a common procedure used all over the ancient Near East. In the time of David foreskins were often taken, but where this was not possible because the enemy was circumcised (as it seems the Midianites were) a hand would be taken instead. This was also a common Egyptian practice. The Assyrians had a penchant for cutting off the heads of the dead so that the scribes could count the enemy slain for the record in the royal annals.

The main hand weapon of Joshua's soldiers, as of all armies in the ancient Near East at this time, was the bronze bladed khopesh, a curved sword for slashing.

41

Gideon's campaign was the outcome of careful planning, rapid execution taking advantage of knowledge of the local terrain and a ruthless follow-up. His reward was to be offered the crown by his people:

The men of Israel said to Gideon, 'Rule over us, you and your son and your grandson, since you have rescued us from power of Midian.

(Judges 8:22)

He rejected their offer, on the grounds that 'Yahweh shall rule you', but his 'son' Abimelech was not averse to assuming a royal mantle for himself. His story is a strange yet revealing and significant one.

Abimelech 'The King'

The story of the rise and fall of Abimelech in the *Book of Judges* stands apart from the other accounts concerning those 'called' by Yahweh to save 'his' people. He was *not* called – and strictly speaking he was not even an Israelite.

Thus, his inclusion within the *Book of Judges* may well have served to make a theological point with respect to political power and kingship: in Israel no man could be King unless Yahweh designated him such. The rise and fall of this ruthless individual also gives us a good insight into the reality of relations between the Israelites and their Canaanite neighbours and the degree to which for the greater part of the time following their arrival in Canaan most of the tribes managed to forge some kind of accommodation with the natives and to live in peace with them. They did not live in a state of perpetual warfare.

Offer of Strength

Tradition has Abimelech as the 'son' of Gideon, and he is called in the Biblical text the 'son of Jerrubbaal', which is an alternative title for Gideon; but there is good reason to believe, that there was no relationship between them.

Gideon had seventy sons begotten by him, for he had many wives. His concubine who lived at Shechem, also bore him a son, to whom he gave the name Abimelech.

(Judges 8:31–32)

What this probably implies is that some kind of special relationship existed between the tribe of Manasseh and the people of the city of Shechem. This relationship allowed for intermarriage between the Canaanites and their Israelite neighbours, an occurrence unlikely at a later date. It has been suggested that, far from being an ordinary Shechemite woman, Abimelech's mother was the daughter of one of the ruling Canaanite aristocracy of the city, which would account for his seemingly easy acceptance by the Shechemites as their ruler. Dominating the tribe of Manasseh and thus Shechem also at this time was the clan of Jerrubbaal. The power that the Israelites had over them was not to the liking of the ruling class at Shechem but, until Abimelech presented himself to them with an offer to help reassert Shechemite dominance in the area, albeit on his terms, they could do little about it. What Abimelech offered them may not have been to their liking but it was infinitely preferable to domination by the Israelites. What emerges plainly is the Machiavellian nature of Abimelech, who is prepared to exploit this antipathy for his own ambitious ends. Consider the proposal he puts to the rulers of the city:

Abimelech son of Jerubbaal confronted his mother's brothers at Shechem and to them and to the whole clan of his maternal grandfather's family, he said, 'Please put this question to the leading men of Shechem: Which is better for you: to be ruled by seventy people – all Jerubbaal's sons – or to be ruled by one? Remember too I am your flesh and bone.' His mother's brothers said all this on his behalf to all the leading men of Shechem, and their feelings swayed them to follow Abimelech, since they argued, 'He is our brother'.

When his offer had been accepted Abimelech expected the Shechemites to provide him with the means of procuring the services of soldiers to destroy 'the sons of Jerubbaal.' Entering the temple to Baal-Berith the Shechemites took from the treasury 70 shekels of silver. With this sum Abimelech proceeded to recruit a body of mercenaries who would view him, as their paymaster, as their leader. That such men were available for hiring suggests that conditions in Canaan may well have been much the same in the eleventh and twelfth centuries as they had been at the time of the Amarna letters, when small wars between the city states were fought using mercenary forces hired from amongst the Hapiru. With this mercenary force Abimelech moved rapidly against the Jerubbaal's clan city of Ophrah and there killed all the 'sons of Jerubbaal' save one who managed to escape.

Rule of the Sword

In reward for his action the aristocracy of the city made Abimelech their King, although it began to emerge quite quickly that he aspired to greater things. He may have been spurred on not only by ambition but also by his recognition that in the final analysis his power was at the mercy of his hired mercenaries. Their personal loyalty to him was dubious and in direct proportion to his willingness to reward them. Thus the process of expanding his domain to encompass the rule of the Manassite and Ephraimite clans in the mountains around Shechem was the inevitable consequence of the nature of his rule.

To the Shechemites the revelation that Abimelech was little more than an adventurer intent on carving out a kingdom for himself at their expense led to the emergence of an opposition to his rule. Their grievances were further compounded when Abimelech moved his ruling seat from Shechem to Arumah in Ephraimite territory and installed in

Probable appearance of Hapiru in the thirteenth century B.C. It was the availability of freebooters such as these that allowed Abimelech to raise his own 'private' army.

Shechem an official to govern the city in his name. Deciding that Abimelech could no longer be trusted, the Shechemites charged Abimelech with disloyalty and gathered a force to challenge him. Moving quickly, Abimelech brought his mercenary forces to Shechem and attacked it.

Battle of Shechem

The description of Abimelech's taking of the city gives us a good insight into the techniques employed in the twelfth and eleventh centuries B.C for the reduction of fortified settlements:

All that day Abimilech attacked the town. He stormed it and slaughtered the people inside, razed the town and sowed it with salt.

The attack of Shechem opens with a battle outside the walls of the city, with Abimelech's mercenary troops attacking in three units – the standard procedure of the time for the deployment of troops for battle. Two units hid in the fields, waiting for the Shechemites to deploy their forces in front of the city walls. These units were dispatched to pin down and destroy the enemy while he with the remaining troops under his command headed to the city to prevent the gates being closed and to gain a quick access to the city itself. The Shechemite forces were caught by surprise and destroyed in detail as they attempted to deploy into line, one of the moments of maximum vulnerability for any army. Abimelech's forces then broke in to the city itself, having taken the city gate, the point of greatest weakness in the outer wall defences. Those of the citizens who had managed to escape the blades of Abimelech's mercenaries, some one thousand in all, made their way to the inner citadel of the city, which was also the temple of the god Baal-Berith.

Archaeological excavations of the site of Shechem, identified with Tell Balatah to the east of the modern town of Nablus, have revealed a building some 69 feet by 86 feet which is thought to be the house of Baal-Berith. Like other Canaanite temples, the House of Baal was built in the form of a fortified tower. Such buildings are depicted on Egyptian wall reliefs of Ramesses II in the Ramesseum and show a formidable defensive structure with crenellated walls on four sides allowing the defenders to rain down stones, spears and arrows on any attackers crossing the open ground around the tower.

The problem of taking a building like this was solved by Abimelech:

He went up Mount Zalmon with all his men. Then taking an axe in his hands, he cut off the branch of a tree and put it on his shoulder, and said to the men with him, 'Hurry and do what you have seen me do.' Each of his men similarly cut off a branch; then following Abimelech, they piled all the branches

(*Judges* 9:48–49)

Then, under cover of their shields, they piled the branches against the

gate of the citadel and set fire to this huge bonfire, burning to death all of those inside.

There could be no doubting now that there existed no warrant or legitimacy for Abimelech's rule except through the sword. The very nature of his power thus required a continual resort to force to maintain his position and it was in the act of attacking another city that he met his death, in a manner so demeaning that it became a byword for military incompetence in Israel.

Death in Dishonour

The death of Abimelech occurred in circumstances almost identical to those at Shechem. In this case the town under siege was Thebez, possibly

Based upon a relief from Karnak (now believed to date from the time of Merneptah's campaign in Canaan) this fortified city must have typified major settlements throughout Canaan into the time of the Judges.

the same settlement as that on the border of Neapolis mentioned by the Roman writer Eusebius.

In the middle of the town there was a fortified tower in which all the men of the town took refuge. They locked the door behind them and climbed to the roof of the tower and attacked it. As he was approaching the door of the tower to set it on fire, a woman threw down a millstone on his head and cracked his skull.

(*Judges* 9:50–53)

But Abimelech had no taste for dying an ignominious death, by the hand of a woman. He appealed to his armour bearer:

Draw your sword and kill me, so that it will not be said of me that 'A woman killed him'. His armour bearer ran him through, and he died. When the men of Israel saw that Abimelech was dead, they dispersed to their homes.

(*Judges* 9:54–55)

Alas, he could not escape the verdict of posterity. In 2 *Samuel*, we find Joab, David's army commander, sending word back to the King and offering the death of Abimelech as an awful example of military ineptitude:

Why did you go near the town to give battle? Didn't you know that they would shoot from the ramparts? Who killed Abimelech, son of Jerubbaal? Wasn't it a woman who dropped a millstone from the ramparts, causing his death at Thebez?

(*2 Samuel* 11:20–21)

46

With Abimelech's death the arrangement between Shechem and Manasseh returned to what it had been before his attempt to carve out for himself a kingdom. He left behind no lasting achievement and, while he was the first man in Israel to be called a king, in no way did his example influence the emergence of the Kingship in Israel under Saul. His place then in the *Book of Judges* is hard to understand, for far from being a saviour of his people he was nothing more than a military adventurer.

The Ultimate Enemy

The struggle and conflicts continued. Yet one recurring theme began to be dominant in the warring and fighting. Of all the enemies faced by the Hebrew tribes in the time of the Judges, none could match the efficiency, vigour and ruthlessness of the Philistines.

Having been settled in the coastlands of the Palestinian Shephelah by Ramesses III, following their abortive attempt to invade Egypt in 1186 B.C., these highly organised groups of the 'Sea Peoples' posed a threat of a profound nature to the very existence of the tribes of Israel.

It was out of the Philistine threat to Israel that the nascent movement to a more effective and centralised political structure began to evolve. In time, it was the Philistine menace, moving inland from the coast into the Hebrew heartland, that was to see the emergence of the monarchy under Saul and David. It was a process that was to transform the tribes of Israel into a nation.

Recoiling from the defeat inflicted on them on the border of Egypt by Ramesses III in 1186 B.C., the Sea Peoples settled in Canaan. Based upon the Hedinet-habu relief, this depiction of a group of Sea People as prisoners includes (second figure on the right) a Philistine. Of all the enemies of Israel, they posed the greatest threat to their existence. Their predatory attacks on the lands of the Hebrew settlement provided the catalyst for the emergence of the monarchy under Saul and David.

The Stela of Merneptah

Placing any accurate date on Joshua's invasion of Canaan with the tribes that comprised 'The House of Joseph' is difficult. There is only one source extant prior to the ninth century B.C. that mentions 'Israel' by name. This is the famous granite 'Israel Stela' of the Pharaoh Merneptah, which purports to record his victories in Canaan early in his reign.

There is general agreement that the stela itself was inscribed in the fifth year of the Pharaoh's reign. But there is no consensus as to the year of his succession, suggested dates ranging from 1238 B.C. to about 1213 B.C. The consensus is that the stela makes reference to an Egyptian punitive campaign by Merneptah (or his son) in Canaan, after the death of his father Ramesses II, sometime in the last three decades of the thirteenth century B.C.

From the names on the stela it is possible to see that after following the route of the coastal route, the Egyptian forces moved, in turn, against the cities of Ashkelon and Gezer. They then moved inland into the hill country. There, to the south of Yenoam, which was also named, the army of the Pharaoh came to grips with the forces of 'Israel'. The stela text is written in hymnic form:

> Plundered is Canaan with every evil;
> Carried off is Ashkelon; seized upon is Gezer;
> Yanoam is made as that which does not exist;
> Israel is laid waste, his seed is not;
> Hurru is become a widow for Egypt!
> All lands together they are pacified;
> Everyone who is restless, he has been bound.

Of greatest significance is that 'Israel' is preceded by a hieroglyphic sign used to designate 'a people' – indicating the presence of a wandering or tribal group. Of course, Joshua and his invading tribes were fighting against the Canaanites. But the Egyptians, if indeed they did encounter them, were not likely to have made much distinction between warring groups among the general dissident activity that the expedition had been sent to suppress.

The Bible gives no hint of any encounter between the Israelites and the army of the Pharaoh and some scholars see no significance in this 'encounter' of Egypt with 'Israel', suggesting that the tribes involved were those who had been settled in Canaan for many centuries. But it seems much more reasonable to infer that the Egyptians *did* come into contact with a group of nomadic tribes collectively known as 'Israel' – the very people being led by Joshua.

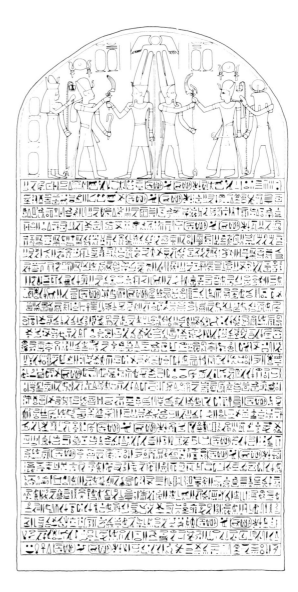

48

Chronology of Events

Whilst it is not possible to give dates in such a chronology with any real certainty, the following represents a feasible and realistic time scale of the main events. However, it has to be noted that some sources place the Joseph narratives much later.

1900–1700 B.C.	Likely period of the Patriarchs.
1720–1580 B.C.	Rule of the Hyksos in Egypt.
1580–1567 B.C.	Possible time of Joseph in Egypt.
1560–1200 B.C.	Canaan under domination of Egypt.
1270–1260 B.C.	Likely time of the Exodus.
1230–1207 B.C.	Merneptah Stela; evidence of Israel in Egypt.
1210–1190 B.C.	Probable 'invasion' of Canaan by 'House of Joseph' under Joshua.
1186 B.C.	Ramesses III defeats 'Sea Peoples' on Egypt's borders; Philistines begin settlement of Palestinian coastal plain.
1150–1050 B.C.	Probable period of the Judges.

Bibliography

Aldred, C. *The Egyptians* Thames and Hudson, 1987.

Anderson, B. *The Living World of the Old Testament*, Longman, 1976.

Bright, J.A. *History of Israel*, 3rd Edition, Philadelphia, 1981.

Edwards, I.E.S. (ed) *Cambridge Ancient History*, Vol. 1 (part 2B) Vol. 2 (parts 1 and 2A), Cambridge University Press, 1971, 1973 and 1975.

Ferrill, A. *The Origins of War* Thames and Hudson, 1986.

Finegan, J. *Archaeological History of the Ancient Middle East*, Dorset, 1979.

Grant, M. *The History of Ancient Israel*, Weidenfeld & Nicolson, 1984.

Jagersma, H.A. *History of Israel in the Old Testament Period* SCM, 1982.

Kitchen, K.A. *Pharaoh Triumphant* Aris and Phillips, 1982.

Miller, M.J. and Hayes, J.H. *A History of Ancient Israel and Judah* SCM, 1986.

Negev, A (ed) *The Archaeological Encyclopedia of the Holy Land* Nelson, 1986.

Noth, M. *The History of Israel* SCM, 1958.

Pritchard, J. *The Ancient Near East*, Vols 1 and 2, Princeton, 1958 and 1975.

Pritchard, J. (ed) *The Times Atlas of the Bible* Times Books, 1987.

Sandars, N.K. *The Sea Peoples* Thames and Hudson, 1978.

Stillman, N. & Tallis, N. *Armies of the Ancient Near East* Wargames Research Group, 1984.

Time-Life Books *The Israelites* Time Life Books, 1975.

Yadin, Y. *The Art of Warfare in Biblical Lands* International Publishing Co., 1963.

King David

WARLORD OF ISRAEL

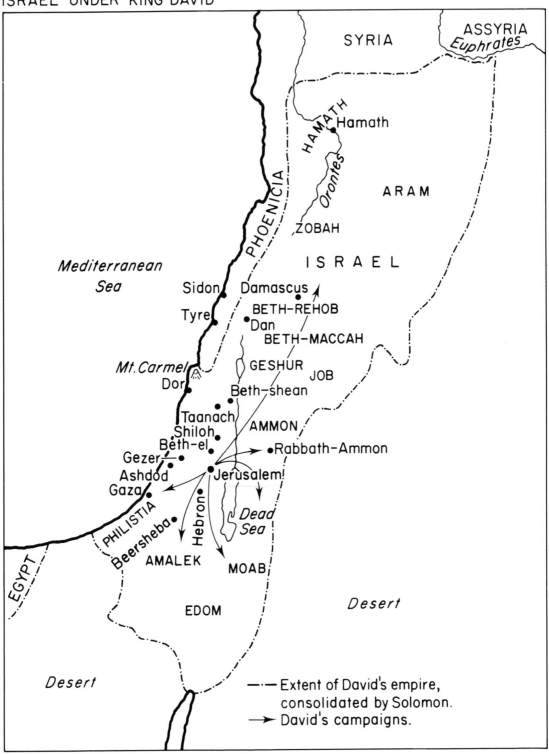

ASSYRIA
Euphrates

SYRIA

HAMATH
●Hamath

ARAM

PHOENICIA

Orontes

ZOBAH

*Mediterranean
Sea*

I S R A E L

Sidon● ●Damascus↗
Tyre● BETH-REHOB
  ●Dan
  BETH-MACCAH

Mt.Carmel GESHUR JOB
Dor●
  ●Beth-shean
  ●
  ●Taanach
  Shiloh● AMMON
  Beth-el●
Gezer● ● ●Rabbath-Ammon
Ashdod
Gaza● ●Jerusalem!
  ●Hebron *Dead
PHILISTIA Sea*
Beersheba●
EGYPT AMALEK MOAB

EDOM *Desert*

Desert

—·—Extent of David's empire,
  consolidated by Solomon.
→ David's campaigns.

David, Son of Jesse, was King of all Israel. He was King of all Israel for a period of forty years: he reigned at Hebron for seven years, and in Jerusalem for thirty three. He died at a good old age, full of days, riches and honour. Then his son Solomon succeeded him.

(1 Chronicles 29:27–29)

The Most Famous King

There can be few people in the world who have not heard of King David of Israel. His name is known to billions, in one way or another, as a consequence of the rise and spread of three great religious movements, Judaism, Christianity and Islam. David, the son of Jesse, is for the Jewish people the greatest of all their kings. He ushered in Israel's 'golden age', the only time in her long history when Israel was a major power in the *ancient* Near East.

For both Jews and Christians it was from David's descendants that the coming of the Lord's Anointed was prophesied. Indeed, Christian faith maintains that the prophecy of the coming of the Messiah was fully realised some thousand years after David's reign in the person of Jesus of Nazareth.

For the followers of Muhammed and the adherents of Islam, David is one of the twenty-eight named prophets in the Koran. The Psalms, attributed to David in all three traditions, are recognised by Islam as one of the revealed books of Allah.

There can be little doubt one of the principal reasons for David's 'popularity' down the ages is the personal appeal of his character as portrayed in the Biblical texts. Like all great figures of the past, legends have accrued around his name. Nevertheless it is his immediate humanity that still attracts. The Bible presents a character with few inhibitions, both in triumph and failure, when euphoric and when in deep, tragic despair. In ancient literature there exist few parallels to the passage wherein King David hears of the death of his son, in battle against his father's forces, having raised his hand in rebellion against David.

The King shuddered. He went up to the room over the gate and burst into tears; and, as he wept, he kept saying, 'Oh, my son Absalom! My son! My son Absalom! If only I had died instead of you! Oh, Absalom my son, my son!

(2 Samuel 19:4)

Compare this picture of a monarch, stripped of pretension, with the work of some anonymous sculptor in the service of the Assyrian King

53

Assurnasirpal II, who lived about a century later than David. A cold and formal visage gazes out on the world, with an expression devoid of emotion and humanity. It is an expression fixed in an image of monarchy which is the very antithesis to that of David of Israel.

Nevertheless, one must recognise the tendency to accept in David what in others is condemned as naked ambition, treason, rebellion and ruthlessness. For all the qualities we perceive in his person he was still very much a man of his time. It is in his own time, with all of its contingencies, that he has to be placed for any real view of the man.

In the light of the lack of any non-Biblical sources whatsoever concerning the life and times of David, we fall back upon the Bible itself as the principal source. From the historical point of view, this requires us to recognise that we cannot regard in an uncritical light material in the books of *Samuel*, 1 *Chronicles* and part of 1 *Kings*, wherein lies the account of the career of David. In reality, this is to recognise that the traditions concerning David have been chosen and edited to reflect the particular interests of the person or persons concerned in the actual process of drawing up the texts. Thus, it is almost certain that we come to the story of David with a set of interests different from those whose handiwork we now propose to use.

Immediately, there are problems in chronology. We have no certain dates for any events in either the reign of David's predecessor Saul or David himself. However, we will proceed on the assumption that Saul reigned for about twenty years from approximately 1020 B.C. David's reign and that of his son Solomon lasted about seventy years. This places David's reign somewhere between 1000 B.C. and 960 B.C.

We have no way of knowing when he came to Saul's court, but we know that David was the youngest son of Jesse of Bethlehem. Of his early life we know next to nothing, apart from observing that he was born at a time when the whole of Israel was under dire threat from a powerful foe bent on her subjugation. In the last quarter of the tenth century B.C., the threat posed by the Philistines was of such a great order that it took a revolution in the internal politics of the tribal society that was Israel to defeat it. The Philistines were major players in the story of David's rise to power and to the kingship of Israel. Their arrival in the eastern Mediterranean and the establishment of their power has to be understood in providing the backdrop to David's ascendency.

The Sea Peoples

The Philistines made their first recorded appearance on the eastern Mediterranean stage at the beginning of the twelfth century B.C. They

were identified as one of a number of distinct groups designated collectively by the Egyptians as 'The People of the Sea'.

The latter part of the thirteenth century B.C. had seen the beginning of a great convulsion in the long established political and economic order in the eastern Mediterranean lands. The upheaval was caused by a flood of invaders who overwhelmed Anatolia, Syria and Palestine and it was only at the borders of Egypt that this human tide was brought to a halt. There Pharaoh Ramesses III defeated these 'Sea Peoples' in two great battles fought on land and sea. It is from his own account of these events – preserved on the walls of the temple at Medinet Habu that he had built to commemorate his victories – that we can gain a deeper insight into what has been called 'The Great Land and Sea Raids'.

Taken from the wall reliefs at Medinet Habu, a warship of Ramesses III is shown attacking the Sea Peoples. Their boats are out of view, but numerous bodies in the water indicate the Egyptians reaping great slaughter amongst the invaders. On board are prisoners with the 'feathered' headdresses of the Peleset or Philistines.

Ramesses III and the Peleset

Of particular significance was the Egyptian identification of the different groupings making up the enemy forces: 'Their league was Peleset, Tjekker, Shekelesh, Denyen and Weshesh United lands'.

It is now agreed that the Peleset, the first people listed, were the Philistines. That they were listed first may not just have been because they were the most numerous group amongst the land forces advancing on Egypt; the Egyptians knew of them already, as former mercenary soldiers in their employ as garrison troops in Palestine. This would not be inconsistent with the policy of the recruitment of former enemies or the impressment of captured soldiers as 'slave troops' into the Egyptian army. Possibly the most famous of these were the Sherden employed by Ramesses II as part of his personal guard and used by him at the battle of Kadesh against the Hittites; Ramesses III also used such troops.

Archaeological excavations at Beth-Shean, in the northern Jordan valley, have revealed clay anthropoid sarcophagi bearing the characteristic 'feathered' head-dress shown as being worn by the Peleset soldiers on the reliefs at Medinet Habu. Further finds of weaponry and other artifacts linked to the Philistines renders their employment as garrison troops by Ramesses and earlier Pharaohs as virtually certain. Thus, one could describe the Philistines in the Palestine garrisons as a first wave of Sea Peoples who also functioned as a 'Trojan Horse' in the Egyptian employ. In contact with their 'homelands', or at least with their kin, they passed on knowledge of affairs within Palestine such that, when the second wave of invaders entered the land, they threw in their lot with them and marched on Egypt itself.

The land attack was stopped by the Egyptians, but a second attack was launched by sea against the Nile delta. In inscriptions on the temple wall at Medinet Habu, Ramesses says of the attack by sea:

As for those who came together on the sea, the full flame was in front of them at the river mouths, while a stockade surrounded them on the shore. They were dragged ashore, hemmed in and flung down on the beach, their ships made heaps from stern to prow and their goods . . .

The two battles succeeded in foiling the attempt by the Sea Peoples to establish any foothold in Egypt. However, Ramesses was unable or unwilling to force them out of Palestine and so the permanent settlement of the 'Sea Peoples' in Palestine was a consequence of Egypt's tacit acceptance of its inability to compel the newcomers to vacate the land acquired through conquest. The bombast and vainglory of Ramasses' claims may have disguised the reality of a Pyrrhic victory over the Peoples of the Sea:

I extended all the boundaries of Egypt. I overthrew those who invaded them from their lands. I slew the Denyen in their isles, the Tjekker and the Peleset were made ashes.

Egyptian power and influence declined rapidly in Palestine following the death of Ramesses III in 1162 B.C. It meant that a real opportunity arose for the Philistines, still nominally vassals of Egypt, to carve out their own 'empire' in the area, unfettered by any possible intervention from Egypt, the only power that could actually have prevented their doing so.

Philistine warriors from the time of Saul and David would have appeared much as they were depicted in the wall reliefs at Medinet Habu. The characteristic headdress was probably made of reeds, feathers, hair or leather strips, stiffened and dyed. Body armour was either of bronze or leather, with a kilt in bright shades of green, red or blue. Most obvious is the large sword, a most fearsome weapon.

The Philistines in Palestine

Being the dominant group amongst those who were 'defeated' by Ramesses, the Philistines laid claim to the best territory in the land which had been made over to them by the Pharaoh. They occupied the area of the fertile Palestine coastal plain, a strip of land some forty miles long and fifteen to twenty miles at its widest point.

Evidently, a number of cities that Ramesses handed over to the Philistines in due course became the five city states of the Philistine Pentapolis. Three of these were built alongside the Via Maris so were well placed to oversee the passage of trade through Philistia: Ashkelon

The distinctive 'bird headed' prow and stern of the Sea Peoples' vessels. This particular ship is crewed by Philistines, some carrying the long and fearsome iron swords that so impressed the Egyptians.

had the benefit of a harbour; Gaza was also a major commercial centre; Ashdod although first destroyed by the Philistines, was rebuilt and became a major fortress and important commercial centre. Further inland, the remaining two cities of Gath and Ekron were also major fortresses. Further to the north they founded a harbour town at the site of Tell el-Qasile. This allowed them not only to engage in trade with Phoenicia, but also to compete with the Phoenicians for the very lucrative sea trade in the area. Indeed, the constant reference to commercial and trading matters provides a basic clue as to the Philistine ambitions in the area, ambitions that by their very nature would bring them into inevitable conflict with the Hebrew people in the uplands of the Palestinian interior.

The political organisation of the cities of the Pentapolis was oligarchic, each being ruled by a leader known as a Seren. Each Seren ruled over a native Canaanite and Philistine population and they were organised on a feudal basis. A professional military class held fiefs of land from the Seren and in times of war they would be required in fulfilment of their duties as vassals to support their lord. Indeed, David became the vassal of Achish of Gath, who gave the city of Ziklag to him as his fief. In return, David was required to fulfil military duties as required by Achish and would have served as a mercenary vassal at the battle of Mount Gilboa where Saul was killed had not the other Seranim over-ruled Achish for fear of David's loyalty.

In the period following the death of Ramesses III, the Philistines embarked upon a policy of developing and stimulating trade by both land and sea. Acting in concert as a trading confederacy, the Seranim worked through an annual council that determined policy. A unified military command allowed for deployment of forces from all five cities

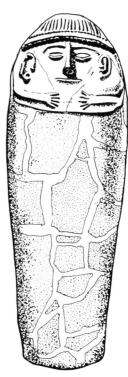

A clay anthropoid coffin of the type discovered during the excavations at Beth-Shean, a Philistine and former Egyptian fortress. The depiction of feathers on the head strongly suggests it housed the body of a Philistine. The dating of the coffin to the twelfth century B.C. means that it was made for a Philistine mercenary in the service of Ramesses III.

in support of common military objectives – usually arising from the need to oversee and protect commercial enterprises the Seranim had embarked upon. Apart from the sea trade already mentioned, the Philistines developed trade links with the desert to the east of the main Hebrew settlement. The continued retention of strategic centres in the plain of Esdraelon, and at Beth-Shean and Succoth in the Jordan valley allowed caravans bearing very extensive trade to reach Philistia. It was partly out of a desire to preserve the security of these trade routes, in the face of attacks upon them by Hebrew tribesmen coming down from the hills, that prompted the Philistines to move their army against the raiders.

However, a major confrontation between Philistines and Hebrews had been inevitable once the former determined that their desire for hegemony over Israel could be realised. The Philistine needs, for security and economic gain, were allied to a legal justification; as masters of southern Palestine, they were the heirs and successors to the Egyptians. In terms of international law, they could lay claim to the whole area, including the lands of the Hebrew settlement, as their own. In their formidable army, they possessed the instrument to translate the desire for hegemony into actuality.

Hebrews and Philistines

It was in the middle of the eleventh century B.C. that major Philistine expansion into Israel began with a drive into the tribal uplands of Ephraim. An important battle took place near the Philistine frontier station at Aphek. A levy of the tribes of Ephraim, Benjamin and Manasseh assembled at Eben-ezer to do combat with the enemy and in an initial battle the Hebrew forces were defeated. In order to raise the morale of the dispirited Hebrew soldiers, the Ark of the Covenant, the very symbol of Israel's covenant with its God, was brought from its sanctuary at Shiloh. It was accompanied to the battlefield with all due ceremony and was carried by the two sons of Eli, the chief priest of the sanctuary. By its presence it was assumed victory over the uncircumcised enemy would be assured.

Alas, whilst the ark certainly raised the morale of the Hebrew levies as intended, it could not compensate for the disciplined ranks of the Philistine soldiery nor the long iron swords that executed so much destruction on Israel that day:

So the Philistines gave battle and Israel was defeated, each man fleeing to his tent. The slaughter was very great; on the Israelite side thirty thousand foot soldiers fell. The ark of God was captured too, and Hophni and Phinehas the two sons of Eli died

(1 Samuel 4:10–11)

Plainly, the number of those killed is greatly exaggerated, as is the case with the reporting of numbers in battles in almost all sources from the ancient period. The removal of one nought gives a more credible total of 3000 dead. For a tribal society of the sort that Israel still was at this stage of its national development, the outcome of the battle was a catastrophe of the first order. The impact of the loss of the ark, the very symbol of their religion sent shock waves through the whole of Israel.

Furthermore, religious beliefs of the time considered that when battle was joined, the god or gods of the respective combatants were party to the conflict – and the outcome of the clash of arms reflected on their power. Therefore, the Philistines saw in this great victory the triumph of their own gods.

Though the ark was returned eventually, in military terms the twin defeat at Eben-ezer opened up the whole of the Hebrew lands to the west of the Jordan to the Philistine forces. Whilst the biblical material gives no systematic account of the Philistine occupation it does indicate sacking of the territory and very harsh rule. The sanctuary at Shiloh was destroyed and military governors were imposed on the people, ruling from hilltop fortresses such as the large one constructed at Gibeah.

A cast from the temple of Ramesses III at Medinet Habu, this Philistine wears the characteristic headress associated with the Peleset or Sea Peoples.

Rule of Iron

From their strongholds Philistine units were despatched to levy the tribute imposed on the Hebrews. Unable to occupy the whole territory for want of numbers, these units also had the task of overseeing the collection from the tribesmen of all weapons with a view to depriving the tribesmen of the means to oppose their Philistine overlords.

As a further means of rendering the conquered territories quiescent, the military governors imposed their 'iron monopoly' on the people. This has often been interpreted as the Philistines consciously depriving the Hebrews of any access to the working of iron and thus denying them the superior weapons on which Philistine domination of Israel was supposedly based. However, such a view draws heavily upon the paradigm of the iron monopoly enjoyed by the earlier Hittite Empire in Anatolia. This would now seem to have been somewhat less effective than was first thought. The upheavals and dislocation caused in the eastern Mediterranean brought about a very serious breakdown in trade and access to traditional sources of raw materials for the manufacture of bronze became highly problematic. In all likelihood, such conditions provided the impetus and incentive for people to look to the working of iron as an alternative to bronze weaponry. Although the use of iron increased in the eleventh century B.C., it was only in the following two centuries that its use increased greatly. The Philistines introduced the use of iron into Palestine on a major scale. Furthermore, its widespread use for weaponry was a significant factor in their military success over the Hebrews. Yet it seems they did not have a monopoly, either on the knowledge of iron or its actual working. Thus, the imposition of a monopoly on the Hebrews seems to suggest a general prevention of manufacture of weapons, including those of iron, in order to enforce internal security. It also ensured that when metal implements such as ploughshares, axes, mattocks and scythes needed to be sharpened, only Philistine blacksmiths could do the job.

It was against this unpromising background that the incentive arose for a new political institution that would allow the Philistine menace to be defeated. The diffuse power of the Hebrew tribal league, conducting affairs within a theocratic framework in which Yahweh, the God of Israel, was the recognised ruler, was no longer viable. A king was needed, who by virtue of the centralised power and authority vested in him and in his office, could unify and liberate the energies and resources of the people to take on the might of the Philistines.

The long, straight sword employed by the Sea Peoples and Philistines and used to great effect against the Egyptians and Israelites. The example opposite was discovered near Beit Dagon in Philistia and dates from the eleventh century B.C.

Kingdom of Saul

The reign of Saul, Israel's first king, ended as it had begun, fighting the Philistines. On the battlefield of Mount Gilboa, surrounded by the bodies of his dead sons, pierced through with arrows and with the enemy closing in on him, he chose to fall on his sword rather than risk the ignominy of capture.

Without doubt he died a tragic figure. Consumed by self-doubt, he nurtured a deep and profound suspicion of the motives and ambitions of his former son in law, who at the time of his death was in the service of his enemies. He felt abandoned by the God who had given him his throne and was afflicted by some deep psychological ill which at once fed on and compounded his fears. Perhaps he sought in the battle of Mount Gilboa a final ending to his problems, a desired and blessed oblivion. Biblical accounts of his rise and fall are the subject of religious expediency and one has to look beyond these to establish a truer picture of his life's path to Gilboa.

Rise to Power

A very real problem in attempting to construct a chronology of Saul and his reign lies in the material in the Bible dealing with him. In the first instance, nearly half of the *First Book of Samuel* in which we find the 'story' of Saul is concerned with the rise of David and seems designed to prepare the reader for his reign – which then forms the substance of the *Second Book of Samuel*. Furthermore, the Biblical editors' treatment of the material concerning Saul strongly suggests that he has fallen victim to the rewriting of 'history'. Clearly, they wished to portray an idealised picture of divine control of the affairs of Israel in the early days of the monarchy. The Biblical account of the rise of David to the kingship of Israel and his portrayal as the 'ideal' monarch, the chosen of Yahweh, is a result of careful selection by the Bible writers. Thus, rather than it providing a true account of Saul's life, material is presented in such a way as to distort his personality. Thus, his story suffers much in the telling.

Nevertheless, it was as the leader of a band of soldiers opposed to the Philistines in the central hill country that Saul emerged on the scene sometime between 1025–1000 B.C. In all probability, his early career was reminiscent of that of the Judges, except that the consequences of his successful military activities led to him being given a crown, such a move arising out of the exigencies of the moment and the need to defeat the Philistine threat.

Saul managed to seize the major Philistine fortress at Gibeah and eject the enemy garrison at Michmash across the valley. The reputation generated by this twin action led the inhabitants of Jabesh-Gilead to appeal to Saul and his 'army' to help them in their desperate plight as Nahash, king of the Ammonites laid seige to their town. Saul requested a muster of troops from 'throughout the territory of Israel', crossed the Jordan, his forces defeating the Ammonites and raising the siege. Having thus achieved a second major victory, and against a different opponent, his qualifications for kingship seemed to be apparent.

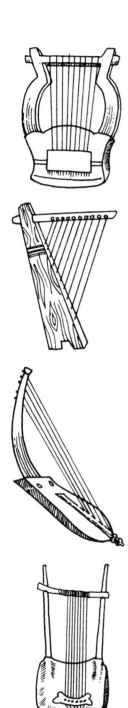

Saul and Samuel

When exactly Saul was declared King is not certain, although it is very possible this was done *before* he crossed the Jordan to relieve Jabesh. Certainly, his request to 'all Israel' implies a degree of status and reputation that suggests he could command the attention of most of the tribes, albeit under a threat of a fairly graphic kind. The mustering request was probably made at an assembly of the people presided over by the reluctant prophet Samuel, whose attitude to the monarchy seems to have been highly equivocal.

It is in his relations with Samuel that the root of Saul's problems lay. Samuel was undoubtedly a figure of great prestige amongst the tribes. As leader of the tribal league, his was the voice most frequently heard before the coming of Saul. In his person the power in the land was unambiguously mediated from a religious perspective. Such prestige and status may well have been difficult for Samuel to give up. The establishment of a monarchy carried with it a momentum of its own, as Samuel himself had warned. As a consequence, he had stated (1 *Samuel* 8:11–18) that Israel would move away from its unique status as a theocracy (literally 'God rules') and become like the other nations.

The establishment of the monarchy required that whoever was king simply had to work out some favourable and practical relation with the national religion and its representatives. Saul failed in this task. In the end, only the genius of David allowed such an accommodation not only to work, but also to serve his own interests. The people of Israel had for so long thought of themselves as a theocracy that there was difficulty placing the idea of a monarch within their religious ideology.

Saul simply could not win; he had no model on which to draw, no previous experience of kingship in Israel to guide him. In his own mind – and in the mind of his people and of Samuel – a secular kingship, outside of the domain of the religion of Israel was simply inconceivable. Had not Samuel, however reluctantly, anointed him and thus publicly declared that although Saul was the chosen of the people it was Yahweh who validated his claim to the crown? Even so, Samuel had also stated that:

If you fear and serve Yahweh and obey his voice and do not rebel against his commands, and if both you and the king who rules you follow Yahweh your God, all will be well. But if you do not obey Yahweh's voice but rebel against his commands, Yahweh's hand will be against you and your king

(1 Samuel 12:12–15)

The corollary of the crown being in the gift of Yahweh was that through the mouthpiece of his prophet he could also take it away and give it to another – which is what seems to have occurred ultimately.

Saul clearly lacked the subtlety to deal with the difficult, testy and sensitive Samuel. No incident better reveals this than the clash between them over the Amalekites. This tribe of bedouin lived in the Negev desert to the south of Beer-Sheba and had been raiding settlements of the

The Israel of David's time pro-hibited any visual art depicting the human form. Consequently, this led to music becoming the main form of artistic expression.

tribe of Judah for plunder. Samuel appeared to Saul and 'through' the prophet Yahweh gave the divine command to utterly destroy the Amalekites, to exterminate them – literally an injunction to Holy War.

Saul put the whole of the Amalekite population to the sword – but saved Agag the king, and the best of the cattle and sheep. Therein lay the sin against which Samuel raged. By not carrying out fully Yahweh's injunction, Saul had disobeyed Yahweh and his failure had a price: 'Since you have rejected Yahweh's word, he has rejected you as king'.

In order that Yahweh's ordained curse of destruction be carried out, Samuel himself fulfilled it by butchering Agag before Yahweh at Gilgal. Thereafter he departed and Saul never met Samuel again.

The effect of rejection by Yahweh played greatly on Saul's mind. In all likelihood, it was the cause of a profound neurosis that began to affect his personality. This was further compounded by the seemingly inevitable rise of a young warrior who had joined his army as a professional soldier. By his success in war, the young David was drawing to himself an adulation and a prestige that seemed to the King, in his suspicion and fear, to feed a limitless ambition that aspired to the throne of the kingdom itself. In the light of earlier observations about the bias in the Biblical material, maybe Saul's fears of David's ambition were not purely the consequence of a growing paranoia. Rather, they were as much based on a genuine perception of the aspirations of the son of Jesse of Bethlehem, a perception which the Biblical editors in their attempt to portray David as the archetypal hero, the chosen of Yahweh and the perfect king, appear to have felt justified in quietly editing out of the material.

Sovereignty of Saul

It would be wrong to think of Saul's 'kingdom' in terms of a centralised monarchy ruling over a distinct territorial domain defined by proper borders. There was constant warfare between Saul's forces and those of his enemies. Apart from the tribal lands of southern Ephraim and Benjamin, the other 'lands' claimed as being under his aegis could only have been so when his forces were actually in the territories concerned. We can best speak of his sovereignty in terms of the loose influence he exerted on territories beyond Ephraim and Benjamin where the people looked to him for protection against their enemies. He was thus able to move through the southern hill country to attack the Amalekites. The degree of support that he could depend upon from the people of this area is well attested to when later he was given assistance and information by them when hunting for David after the latter had turned renegade. Essentially, Saul's military activities were directed towards the prevention of further encroachment and the maintenance of security in the tribal territories under his 'influence'. In a reign of constant military activity, the Philistines were the most persistent and unyielding of his foes.

63

faith enables him to triumph over the seemingly invincible enemy, when the 'professional' soldiers through cowardice or fear, are unwilling to take on such a foe. Additionally, it has common folklore motifs of the rewards of fame, power and the 'hand' of the king's daughter. However, one should be more than a little wary in accepting the historical veracity of the 'Goliath' story at face value. After all, Samuel attributes the killing of Goliath to another:

Again war with the Philistines broke out at Gob, and Elhanan son of Jair, of Bethlehem, killed Goliath of Gath the shaft of whose spear was like a weaver's beam.

(2 Samuel 21:20–21)

Interestingly, Elhanan is identified as one of David's warriors whilst to David himself is attributed the death of an unnamed opponent of 'huge stature' who nevertheless came from Gath in Philistia.

Saul and David

Whatever the validity of the accounts, it seems most likely that David came to the court of Saul as a professional soldier. Within a short time he began to make a name for himself as a great warrior, to such an extent that his own reputation began to outshine that of Saul:

Saul has slain his thousands and David his ten thousands.

(1 Samuel 18:6–7)

It is easy to understand why David's growing fame may have caused Saul some unease. Saul had undoubted aspirations to found a dynasty and his eldest son Jonathan was already being regarded as the heir apparent. Yet the general status of the monarchy and Saul's own particular position were not so certain in the minds of all the people that some other arrangement might not be considered. Saul's own position may itself have been especially ambiguous: whilst many in Israel regarded him as *Melek* or king, those living in the lands where his rule was less certain may still have considered him as something less than a monarch. Saul voiced his fears to his son following Jonathan's efforts to help David escape:

As long as the son of Jesse lives on earth, neither you nor your royal rights are secure

(1 Samuel 20:31)

Nevertheless, prior to the decline in the relationship David seems to have enjoyed a very close relationship with the royal family. A very strong bond grew up between David and Jonathan; and Saul's daughter Michal became David's wife, purchased for the bride price of one hundred Philistine foreskins! It would seem that Saul saw the match between David and Michal as a way of containing the rising young soldier and of harnessing him to the royal cause; but it was not to be.

Saul's fear, jealousy and suspicion, compounded by his rejection by Samuel, became focused on David. Before long, Saul seemed prepared

This harpist, from a Babylonian terracotta plaque circa 2000 B.C., plays the type of instrument David was attributed to have employed to soothe the ill-humour of Saul. Known as a nebel, it was triangular and gut strings were stretched from the sounding board, attached to a supporting cross-piece.

As the battle of Mount Gilboa drew to its tragic end, the Philistines closed in on Saul. With his three sons lying dead around him, he chose death by his own hand rather than the disgrace of capture.

to eliminate the cuckoo living in his nest, and at some point David himself believed it to be expedient to break with Saul. Whilst Saul's attitude was probably a major factor in causing David to flee, the degree to which Biblical narrators appear to go out of their way to continually portray David as the innocent, unwitting victim of this unjustified hatred does not ring true. David was no wide-eyed innocent; he was not always the victim with no cause for suspicion to be attached to his motives. Without doubt he was a very subtle player of the political game with a remarkable ability to exploit situations to his own ends. Also, he was fortunate in having others who would perform the duplicitous acts from which he would benefit and yet not be blamed. The times in which he lived were harsh and savage and he was playing for very high stakes, as Saul rightly suspected. Ambition that aspired to a crown did not and could not shirk from rebellion, collusion with the enemy and the despatch of opponents. Certainly, there was another side to David; the characteristics that caused him to mourn for both Saul and Jonathan after their deaths at Mount Gilboa, that was ready to forgive his son Absalom even after his rebellion against his father. Nevertheless, we do the man no credit to portray him simply as the innocent, devoid of ambition, as the Biblical portrayal of his time in the service of Saul would suggest. Larger than life he may appear, but like the majority of humankind he was neither angel nor demon, just a very liberal synthesis of both.

David the Renegade

Warrior mounted on a camel, an animal being employed in warfare as early as the tenth century B.C. The Amalekites probably used such beasts in their raids on the Hebrew settlements in southern Judah before Saul took positive action against them.

Following his escape from the court of Saul, David made his way to the cult centre of Nob where the priesthood had been relocated following the Philistine destruction of Shiloh. The priesthood was not aware of his flight, nor was David willing to communicate his position to them. Having obtained supplies from Ahimilech the priest, David then made his way to his own tribal territory of Judah and there secured himself a stronghold at Adullam, to the south-west of the Jebusite city of Jerusalem. There he was joined in his cause by a succession of people who had their own grievances against Saul and his regime. One of these was the prophet Gad, who although always a shadowy figure hereafter, stayed with David throughout his career. Another was Abiathar, who remained David's priest until the latter's death and was only dismissed from the royal service by Solomon upon discovery of his part in the conspiracy to place Adonijah on the throne. In fact, these two holy men were the only survivors of a massacre of the priests and other inhabitants of Nob ordered by Saul after he learned of their alliance with David and had assumed that the priesthood itself must be part of David's conspiracy to deprive him of his throne.

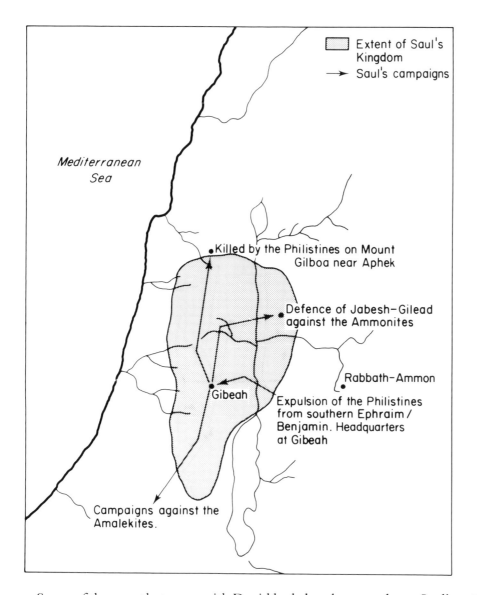

Extent of Saul's Kingdom

Saul's campaigns

Mediterranean Sea

•Killed by the Philistines on Mount Gilboa near Aphek

Defence of Jabesh–Gilead against the Ammonites

•Rabbath–Ammon

Gibeah

Expulsion of the Philistines from southern Ephraim / Benjamin. Headquarters at Gibeah

Campaigns against the Amalekites.

The extent of the Kingdom of Saul with an indication of his main military campaigns.

Some of the men that were with David had also chosen to leave Saul's service; others would have suffered at the expense of the favouritism Saul showed to those of his own tribe of Benjamin. Dispossessed of their lands, which had been given over to the servants of Saul, they had little to lose and perhaps much to gain by throwing in their lot with the rebel. Even amongst those who should have been his undoubted supporters Saul had cause to fear. His appeal to them had little to do with loyalty to his person. It was directed explicitly to their mercenary instincts:

'Listen Benjaminites!' said Saul to them, 'Is the son of Jesse going to give you all fields and vineyards and make you all commanders of thousands and commanders of hundreds that you all conspire against me?

(1 Samuel 22:7)

67

One cannot be sure whether we are here dealing with another example of Saul's paranoia, or with his genuine awareness that support for David was common throughout the army and upper echelons of his regime. Nevertheless, on hearing of David's whereabouts Saul prepared to lead his army south. Fleeing the area around Adullam, David and his followers moved into the wilderness area south-east of Hebron, where Saul with the support and help of the local people continued to search out the rebel. Devoid of support amongst the people who showed a remarkable loyalty to Saul, David and his supporters found their situation becoming very difficult. Indeed many regarded David in a pretty unfavorable light:

Who is David? Who is the son of Jesse? There are many servants nowadays who run away from their masters.

(1 Samuel 25:10–11)

Joining the Enemy

With the countryside loyal to Saul, it was only a matter of time before David's small force was either discovered or betrayed. Consequently, he made a decision that could have ended forever his aspirations to acquire the throne of Israel, had not events turned out otherwise:

One of these days, David thought, I shall perish at the hand of Saul. The best thing I can do is to get away into the country of the Philistines; then Saul will give up tracking me through the length and breadth of Israel and I shall be safe from him. So David set off and went over, he and his six hundred men, to Achish of Gath. He settled at Gath with Achish, he and his men, each with his family and David with his two wives, Ahinoam of Jezreel and Abigail widow of Nabal of Carmel. When news reached Saul that David had fled to Gath, he stopped searching for him.

(1 Samuel 27:1–4)

The Bible does not record the response of his countrymen to the news that David had gone over to the enemy and into the service of Israel's greatest foe.

Exigencies of the moment had left him little choice, but it must have struck David as paradoxical that he should find shelter and safety amongst those whose countrymen he had killed 'in tens of thousands'.

Perhaps there are few better examples to illustrate the observation, coined at another time and in another place, that 'the enemy of my enemy is my friend'.

Duplicitous Service

David thrived in the service of the Philistines. Their willingness to give him status as a vassal with his own fief is as much a testimony to their respect for him as a warrior as it was to their recognition that his defection to them seriously weakened the Hebrew cause.

Achish of Gath, in allocating David the city of Ziklag, laid upon him as part of his vassal responsibilities the protection of south-eastern Philistia where it bordered the hill country of Judah. Furthermore, he would have

been expected to engage on raids on the Jerahmeelite, Judahite and Kenite villages in the hill country. According to Biblical sources, David was in the service of Achish for a year and four months. In that time he was successful in hoodwinking his Philistine overlord into believing he was attacking the Hebrew settlements as commanded. In reality, David was extending his 'protection' of them and gaining great kudos by attacking the settlements of their enemies. Ever the opportunist, he was conducting himself with an eye to the future, but was very careful to cover his deception. Any such duplicity, if discovered by his overlord, would have been ruthlessly dealt with:

David and his men went out on raids against the Geshurites, Gizirites and Amalekites, for these are the tribes inhabiting the region which from Telam, goes in the direction of Shur, as far as Egypt. David laid the countryside waste and left neither man nor woman alive;

Amongst the clay anthropoid coffins found in Palestine, some depict the distinctive Philistine headdress, whilst others do not. In all likelihood, such coffins were a common method of burial amongst garrison troops during this period, be they Egyptian or mercenary soldiers such as the Philistines.

he carried off sheep and cattle, the donkeys, camels and clothing, and then came back to Achish.

(1 Samuel 27:8–10)

By leaving no person alive he covered his tracks most effectively. The extermination of these nomadic 'irritants', and the sharing with villagers of some of the booty gained in the sack of their desert settlements in the hill country, did much to reconcile David in the eyes of Judah.

It was at this time that David learned that the Philistines intended to challenge Saul by compelling him to give battle. It was to be Saul's final scene and David's opening.

Gilboa – Key to a Kingdom

The exact circumstances of the final battle between Saul and the Philistines are not dealt with in the *Book of Samuel*. Nevertheless, it seems that Saul was attempting to wrest from them control of the Jezreel valley with a view to depriving the Philistines of access to Beth-Shean through which caravans from the desert made transit to Philistia.

If Saul was attempting to draw out the Philistines then he had certainly chosen the right place. However, by coming down from the hills to do battle he was fighting the Philistines on ground of their own choosing. The valley provided ideal conditions for deployment of their own chariots and those of their Canaanite allies.

It was whilst the Philistine army was assembling at Aphek that the other rulers, the Seranim, demanded that David and his men take no part in the battle, 'in case he turns on us once the battle is joined'. So, David and his men returned to Ziklag, no doubt relieved not to take part in the spilling of Hebrew blood on the slopes of Mount Gilboa.

The outcome was inevitable:

The Philistines gave battle to Israel, and the Israelites, fleeing from the Philistines, fell and were slaughtered on Mount Gilboa. The Philistines bore down on Saul and his sons and they killed Jonathan, Abinadab and Malchishua, Saul's sons. The fighting grew fiercer around Saul; the archers came upon him, and he was severely wounded by the archers. Saul then said to his armour bearer, 'Draw your sword and run me through with it; I do not want these uncircumcised men to come and make fun of me'. But his armour bearer was very much afraid and would not do it. So Saul took his own sword and fell on it. His armour bearer seeing that he was dead, fell on his sword too and died with him. Thus died Saul, his three sons and his armour bearer, together on the same day. When the Israelites who were on the other side of the Jordan saw that the Israelites had been routed and that Saul and his sons were dead, they abandoned their towns and fled. The Philistines then came and occupied them.

(1 Samuel 31:1–7)

The Philistines, unable to vent their spleen on his living body for the defeats he had inflicted on them:

70

[they] cut off his head and, stripping him of his armour, had these carried round the territory of the Philistines to proclaim the good news to their idols and their people. They put his armour in the temple of Astarte; and his body they fastened to the walls of Beth Shean.

(1 Samuel 31:8–10)

Yet, even in death Saul could still command the respect of those whom he had protected. A group of men from Jabesh-Gilead, remembering with what despatch Saul had marched to their aid when faced with dire peril, stole up to the walls of Beth-Shean and rescued the decapitated bodies of Saul and his sons, left as they were to rot as a testament to the power of Philistine arms. Gently carrying them back, they gave them proper burial underneath the Tamarisk tree at Jabesh.

Tradition has ascribed to David the verses which follow. This is not at all certain, although the sentiments expressed, particularly for Jonathan, would seem to make the claim a credible one. Whoever the author, none in Israel could fail to perceive that a mighty power had gone from the land:

> *Saul and Jonathan, beloved and handsome,*
> *were divided neither in life, nor in death.*
> *Swifter than eagles were they,*
> *stronger than lions.*
>
> *O daughters of Israel, weep for Saul*
> *who gave you scarlet, and fine linen to wear,*
> *who pinned golden jewellery*
> *on your dresses!*
>
> *How did the heroes fall*
> *in the thick of battle?*
>
> *Jonathan for your dying I am stricken,*
> *I am desolate for you, Jonathan my brother.*
> *Very dear you were to me,*
> *your love more wonderful to me*
> *than the love of a woman.*
>
> *How did the heroes fall*
> *and the weapons of war succumb!*
>
> (2 Samuel 1:17–27)

King of Judah

None among Saul's surviving descendants could supply the leadership and thus stave off the Philistines overrunning his kingdom. Abner was Saul's uncle and the army commander. Abandoning the territory to the west of the Jordan he assumed the leadership and arranged for the successful transfer of the capital from Gibeah in Benjamin to Mahanaim. There he installed and thus imposed on Israel a new king, of the family of

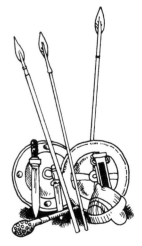

Shields, swords and spears typical of the weaponry and equipment used by the armies of Saul and David.

71

Saul, by the name of Ishbaal (or Ishbosheth). It is difficult to establish Ishbaal's exact relationship to Saul. Whilst 2 *Samuel* 2:8 speaks of him as Saul's son he is never spoken of as such elsewhere in *Samuel* where Saul's sons are specifically named. He may well have been a grandson of Saul and perhaps still a minor, which would then explain the ease with which Abner was able to dominate him. Certainly, Abner was the power behind the throne and Ishbaal a mere figurehead, serving only to legitimise the decisions Abner made in the king's name.

Meantime, having sought the permission of his Philistine masters, David transferred his seat from Ziklag to Hebron. There, and in accord with the wishes of his overlords, David was crowned King of Judah. It was fortunate that the Philistine desire to see David as King of Judah – so as to perpetuate the divisions in the Hebrew ranks – also allowed him to embark upon the path that would allow him to realize his ambition of securing the crown of a united Israel. That such was patently his objective can be ascertained from his message to the people of Jabesh-Gilead commending them for the brave recovery of the bodies of Saul and his sons and concluding 'and now take courage and be men of valour. Saul your lord is dead, but the House of Judah has anointed me king.'

David never even mentioned the name of Ishbaal, clearly feeling him to be an irrelevancy. In appealing to the people to be of courage because he had been crowned King of Judah, David revealed unambiguously where his 'treasure' lay. It was a message from a man confidently in sight of his goal, a letter from a man who would be king over all Israel.

David was King in Hebron for seven years and six months, and all the while still the vassal of the Philistines. In that time conflict had broken out between his forces and those of Ishbaal and continued for much of the period. Although David's forces were already moving into Saulite territory, no other 'battles' in this war are described apart from one ritualised combat that took place at Gibeon. Champions were chosen from amongst the opposing forces in order to settle the confrontation and avoid a general battle. Yet not one of the twelve men from either side survived their respective duels. A mêlée then developed in which Asahel, the brother of Joab and commander of David's forces, was killed by Abner, thus invoking upon himself a blood vengeance whose consequences were to be felt later.

Following a dispute with Ishbaal, Abner determined to abandon the King and secretly opened negotiations with a view to coming to some accommodation with David. For his part, David demanded the return of Michal, his former wife, whom Saul had given to another when David turned rebel. David needed Michal to legitimise his claim to the throne of Israel. However, as a consequence of protocol, such a decision could only be made by Ishbaal as King; Michal was still a princess and of the House of Saul, of which Ishbaal was nominally the head. Completely unaware of the negotiations going on between David and Abner behind his back, Ishbaal readily acquiesced to David's request. Abner managed to secure agreement from both the elders of Israel and the Benjaminites, who were being asked to depose a man from their own tribe. After all, Saul had told 'his' Benjaminites that the son of Jesse would give them neither land nor positions of authority within his kingdom. Whatever David's promise to them as counter to this, it clearly convinced them; Abner came to David at Hebron and informed him 'everything that had been agreed by Israel and the House of Benjamin'.

Abner thus confirmed that David's willingness to ensure the Benjaminite land rights granted by Saul and his retention of their services once he became king was enough to persuade them to David's cause. What then was Abner's price for the betrayal of Ishbaal his king? Almost certainly David's assurance of a very high position in the land when he became King of Israel.

David gave a feast for Abner, who then left for Mahanaim in order to 'rally all Israel to my lord the king, so that they will make an alliance with you, and you will reign over all that you desire'.

However, hearing that Abner was being allowed by David to return, Joab sent his men in pursuit. By a clever ruse, they brought him back to Hebron and it was there that Joab killed him with a ruthlessness that was to become Joab's trademark:

When Abner reached Hebron, Joab took him aside in the town gate, as if to have a quiet word with him, and there struck him a mortal blow in the belly to avenge the blood of his brother Asahel.

(2 Samuel 3:27–28)

Patently, Joab had much to fear by the defection of Abner to David's cause. So, while this murder did indeed honour the requirement of the blood feud, it also eliminated a possible rival. But David's reaction was to condemn utterly the action and his performance was very convincing:

That day, all the people and all Israel understood that the king had no part in the murder of Abner, the son of Ner

(2 Samuel 3:37)

Thus, whilst David called down a curse on the House of Joab, he did nothing more to harm him. Perhaps, in the end, Joab proved too useful for the King to dispose of his services.

Significantly the most important observation in the above is the phrase 'all Israel understood' in respect of David having no part in Abner's murder. There existed by then little to stop the power and the crown being transferred to David. Only the person of Ishbaal himself stood in David's way and his continued existence proved to be most difficult. David was, however, a very lucky man. As so often before in his career, fate intervened to help. Very conveniently, Ishbaal suddenly ceased to be a problem. Two of his chieftains determined to kill him, both to avenge a wrong done to them and their kin by Saul, and also to ingratiate themselves with David:

The description of Goliath's equipment speaks of him carrying 'a scimitar.' The nearest type of weapon of the period to this description was the familiar khopesh, a sickle type sword, with its blade designed for slashing. It would have been used in most of the violent clashes and killings that form part of the story of David's reign.

73

The sons of Rimmon of Beeroth, Rechab and Baanah, set out; they came to Ishbaal's house at the hottest part of the day when he was taking his midday rest. They struck him and killed him, then cut off his head and, taking the head with them, travelled all night by way of the Arabah. They brought Ishbaal's head to David at Hebron

(2 Samuel 4:5–8)

David ordered their execution and had Ishbaal's head buried in Abner's grave.

Throne of Union

A short time later, the elders of the northern tribes of Israel offered David the throne. In Hebron, he made a covenant with them in which they devolved to him the command of the army and the right to call out the tribal levy. Significantly, David did not become king of one united state. Rather he was king over two tribal communities; the northern of Israel and the southern of Judah, who became united only in his person. Israel had covenanted with David that he be their King and Judah had done the same. In order to cement his union with Israel and Judah, David began the search for a new capital. His masterful choice of Jerusalem, lying outside the territory of either tribal confederation, became the ever-present symbol of David's special relationship with those he ruled. It was, and always has been, his city – the 'City of David'.

City of David

No act by David better illustrates his political acumen than the establishment of Jerusalem as his capital city. He had set before himself the objective of bringing the tribes together with a view to limiting their powers and concentrating power on the throne and in his person. However, he was very conscious of the degree to which the northern tribes identified themselves with the House of Saul. They also knew how he had acquired the crown by exploiting the very same, narrow, sectional interests to be found amongst the southern tribes of Judah. Jerusalem lay in neutral territory, between the southern border of the northern tribes and the northern border of the southern tribes. Choosing it as his city illustrated clearly the degree to which David wanted his throne and kingship to be above and transcending all tribal jealousies and claims. However, political foresight preceded physical acquisition.

Conquest of Jerusalem

At the time of David's decision, Jerusalem was still in the hands of the Jebusites, who ruled it independently. The city was built on Mount Ophel, had been extensively fortified and was surrounded by a very thick wall. It was behind this wall, believing themselves impervious to

assault, that the Jebusites sheltered when David's forces came to take the city. From its battlements, the inhabitants hurled abuse at attempts to storm the walls: 'You will not get in here. The blind and the lame will hold you off', believing their city to be so strong that even the weakest could defend it. Alas, the poor Jebusites had not recognized the cunning or determination of their attackers, for the city was taken in a remarkable manner.

The Biblical account is open to various interpretations, but a conventional translation of the word *sinnor* has yielded up the word 'gutter', thought to refer to a water shaft or tunnel. Whatever it may have been, it allowed the attackers, led by Joab, to enter the city surreptitiously. A diversionary attack on the walls distracted the defenders as Joab and his men emerged from the water tunnel and rapidly took the city.

Wall relief carving from the Neo-Hittite settlement of Tell Halef depicting a spearman with a shield. Whilst the relief is quite crude, nevertheless it displays well the footsoldier of David's time.

75

From that day, Jerusalem has been known as the 'City of David'. Very soon after its capture a building programme was under way to transform the former Jebusite fortress into a city fit to be both the capital of Israel and the centre of the nation's religious cult.

The Ark in the City

In bringing the Ark of Yahweh to Jerusalem, David raised the city to the rank of 'metropolis', the centre of the religious cult in the land. He did this for a number of reasons, not the least being to show that his administration in Jerusalem was the heir both to the political and religious traditions of Israel and Judah as well as being the heir to the Kingdom of Saul. The transfer of the Ark focused attention on David as the 'protector' of the cult, now moved from its former home at Shiloh following its destruction by the Philistines. The entrance of the Ark into Jerusalem was accompanied by David's evident exultation and delight, but behaviour which earned him his wife's contempt and rebuke:

> Now as the ark of Yahweh entered the city of David, Michal daughter of Saul was watching from the window and when she saw King David leaping and whirling round before Yahweh, the sight of him filled her with contempt. Much honour the king of Israel has won this day, making an exhibition of himself under the eyes of his servant-maids, making an exhibition of himself like a buffoon!
>
> (2 Samuel 7:16–17)

David told Michal that he had danced for Yahweh and not for the people. Yahweh had chosen him in preference to Saul and his family as leader of Israel and of Yahweh's people.

As ever, David was not slow nor averse to using such sentiment to put abroad an interpretation of his monarchy in religious terms. Out of such ideas emerged the view that Yahweh had blessed the throne of David. The prophet Nathan, attached to David's court, declared that Yahweh had established the throne of David and his house forever, a prophecy whose import would echo down through the centuries.

Force of Arms

The army which David used to forge an empire was composed of two separate formations – the regular standing army, and the militia based on the tribal levies. Whilst most operations were conducted using the professional units, occasions arose where the full tribal levy (or at least selected units from them) would be required to serve alongside the regular forces, as in the second battle against the Aramaean forces of Aram-Zobah at Helam.

The Regulars

The regular army was composed of soldiers from two distinct back-

grounds, one Hebrew and the other foreign. The former had been acquired by David in the course of his rise to power; many had shared his hardships when on the run from Saul and had joined him in the service of the Philistines at Ziklag. According to 1 *Samuel* 22 these numbered initially some 400 men although this later rose to 600 in total. Collectively, this retinue was known as the *Gibborim* or the 'Mighty Men'. From them, David chose an élite group of officers who were designated 'The Thirty'. With himself as its head, this élite formed a supreme army council responsible for determining appointments and promotions, military regulations and other military matters. They also functioned as the permanent commanders of the militia units.

Emulating other monarchs in the Ancient Near East, David recruited into his personal bodyguard foreign mercenary soldiers. Like those of Ramesses II and III, many mercenaries were drawn from the ranks of the 'Sea Peoples', who retained a formidable reputation as warriors. Of particular interest were the Cherethites and the Pelethites, descendants of Cretan warriors who had settled in the Palestinian Shepheleh and were later absorbed by the Philistines.

A scene from the movie King David *which captured successfully the general appearance of the infantry soldiers forming the bulk of David's standing army. They are more representative of the Hebrews than of the mercenary troops, who retained many aspects of their native weapons and costume.*

77

Large numbers of Philistine soldiers served with David's forces. The very strong bond that seems to have grown up between Achish, the Seren of Gath, and David may well have survived the decline in Philistine fortunes and David's accession to the kingship of Israel. The city of Ziklag, given by Achish to David, became crown property. Some six hundred Gittites, as the Philistine inhabitants of Gath were named, served with David under their own commander, whose name was Ittai. It would seem that Ittai was highly regarded by David; during the rebellion of Absalom, he was entrusted with the command of one-third of David's army in the battle with the rebel forces in the forest of Ephraim.

Other nationalities mentioned as serving in David's army included Hittites. Indeed, David procured the death of Uriah, one of the Hittite mercenaries, in order to marry Bathsheeba. The Hittites most likely came from the area around Carchemish in northern Syria.

Plainly, the Eastern Mediterranean offered many opportunities for a warrior ready to sell the services of his sword. The whole of the Near East and not just Israel was always in some state of conflict. Thus there was always a need for professional soldiers and always a ready supply of volunteers.

The essence of the professional army was that in the end they could be trusted to stand by David, both as their leader and as their former brother in arms – and in the case of the mercenaries, as their paymaster.

The Militia

From its early days as a rather primitive tribal levy, David's militia army was developed into a remarkably efficient and well-organized fighting force. It was organised on the basis of twelve divisions, each containing 24,000 men. With the development of a centralized administration, it became possible to organize the divisions on a non-tribal basis. This was important, for the tribes were of different sizes and particular tribes were renowned for their expertise with particular weapons. However, sub-units within each division had a common tribal identity with the balance of arms in each division preserved by each tribe having twelve units available for monthly duty at least once in the year.

Thus, the militia was organised in advance, with permanent units available. Obviously, the size of the units of the larger tribes was greater than those of the smaller. Even so, David could call on a minimum of 24,000 men per month, organised and ready to fight alongside the regular soldiers. At a time of great crisis the whole militia could be called out. As the scope of David's wars increased and as the need to provide more troops to garrison towns also expanded, the militia came to play an increasingly important role. This was a development that did nothing to increase the militia's popularity with the regular soldiers and particularly with the senior officers such as Joab, commander of the army.

Apart from the spear and shield, the bow and sling were the main projectile weapons used for longer range fire. The rams horn, or shafer, was the signalling device before and during battle.

Arms and Equipment

Most of the battles fought by Saul against his enemies had been defensive and fought principally in the hill country occupied by the Hebrew tribes. Thus, most of the battles were fought by infantry in close combat, preceded by missile fire from bows and slings.

The sling was a highly effective weapon in the hands of an expert, as Goliath discovered to his cost. Although essentially a simple weapon, it could outrange by a considerable margin any javelin, the main projectile

In this relief from Tell Halef, the slinger is about to let loose his stone in the direction of the enemy. Its very existence is testimony to the importance of the sling as a weapon around the tenth century B.C.

weapon of the Philistines. It seems also to have been a natural weapon for hill folk, requiring negligible technology in its manufacture, and would have been the ideal weapon for shepherds employed to look after sheep in wild country still inhabited by lions and other vicious predators. Thus, in the task of defending their animals, hill tribesmen became highly effective marksmen with a weapon that could fire a stone with such high velocity that it could easily kill a man. The experienced slinger would do as David is attributed to have done in his contest with Goliath when he:

selected five smooth stones from the river bed and put them in his shepherd's bag

(1 Samuel 17:40)

Smooth stones are aerodynamically efficient; they do not tumble in flight and so the velocity imparted by the sling is not dissipated as the stone moves through the air. Consequently, this velocity is translated into a great deal of kinetic energy upon striking the target. The sling's worth as a weapon seems to have taken some time to be appreciated by 'flatlanders' such as the Philistines. It is not altogether impossible that some of Saul's victories over the Philistines owed much to the effectiveness of his slingers.

Under David, the army would have begun to be equipped from more central weapons shops in the service of the state, although the militia would have depended heavily upon the work of their local metalworkers to provide swords and spears. It will be recalled that it was for this very reason that the Philistines deprived the Israelites of access to native blacksmiths.

Uniforms were certainly unlikely, although the regular soldiery would have had access to body armour of a scale type.

The principal weapons of the infantry would still have been the bow, sling, spear and sword. Interestingly, the Bible (2 *Samuel*) speaks of Joab killing Absalom with 'three darts', that is throwing sticks whose tips are of weighted and sharpened metal. This was plainly a short-range weapon that may have been stored until use on the back of the shield.

There is little to suggest that horses were available in large numbers to provide a cavalry arm and where mobility was needed it seems that mules sufficed. However, the most interesting question we can ask about David's army is did he possess chariots? There are several works which answer without hesitation in the negative. However, in illustrating herein the battle of Helam, David's forces are deliberately portrayed employing chariots. The case for stating that David must have possessed a small chariot force is worthy of consideration. One must first examine the source most frequently invoked to argue that David's army possessed *no* chariots:

David captured one thousand chariots, seven thousand charioteers from Hadadezer and twenty thousand foot soldiers from him. David hamstrung all the chariot teams, keeping only a hundred of them.

(1 Chronicles 18:4–5)

David danced before the Ark processing through Jerusalem's streets. This earned him the contempt of his wife Michal, but was a masterstroke in fusing political and religious life, under his protection, in the 'City of David'.

In fact, this passage is certainly capable of more interpretations than that he hamstrung the horses simply because he neither possessed nor needed chariots of his own. The logic of this particular inference is very dubious. The value of the chariot lay not only in its mobility, but also in its employment as a shock weapon. The common assumption of all armies employing them was that chariots were excellent for running down infantry – where the infantry had not first run away, having taken fright when the chariots charged. In the Ancient World infantry found defence against massed chariot attacks very difficult. Whilst it was possible for them to adopt some form of defence (such as Alexander the Great's instruction to his infantry in dealing with the Persian chariots at Gaugamela), it presupposed infantry highly trained, highly disciplined and prepared to receive the onslaught. Naturally, the commander of any predominantly infantry based army would not choose a battlefield eminently suitable for the enemy to employ his chariots. Such a choice was not always available, inasmuch as an enemy might very well have dictated the choice of the battlefield. Furthermore, it was generally accepted that the best defence against a chariot was another chariot; at Helam, Hadadezer's army disposed of a large number of chariots. So, it is highly unlikely that David could have triumphed over so powerful a foe unless he also had chariots. One can only conclude therefore that David hamstrung the horses because he already had a sufficient number of his own once he had taken one hundred of those captured from the enemy.

In addition to the numerous accounts which refer to forms of single combat, others – whilst not highly detailed – deal with full-scale battles such as Mount Gilboa and Helam. However there are also indirect references to sieges. During Sheba's revolt, the Bible describes how Joab and the professional soldiers, having cornered the rebel after a long pursuit, began:

Characteristic features of the chariots employed by the army of David and those of the Aramaean forces of Aram-Zobah. The horse is protected with scale armour, with extra padding underneath the wooden yoke saddle. The archer also wears scale armour and his ready supply of arrows was backed up with a javelin. Such chariots provided the principal shock weapons of armies at the time – but only when such forces were within the economic resources of the state.

David's chariots rode down Hadadezer's panicking troops in the Battle of Helam, the victory over powerful Aram-Zobah which gave him complete control of TransJordan.

Laying siege to him in AbelBeth-Maacah, they threw up a ramp against the outer wall of the town, while the whole army accompanying Joab undermined the walls to bring it down.'

(2 Samuel 20:15–16)

Plainly, the process of laying siege to a fortified town was well understood by David's men. They threw up a ramp against the outer wall with the intention of using it to gain entrance to the town. Assault via the ramp was probably combined with collapse of the walls, whose foundations were already mined elsewhere. But this was an assault only upon the outer wall; within it lay the inner wall. Abel Beth Maacah was a formidably protected site. In the territory of the tribe of Dan, on the very northern border of Israel, it functioned as a garrison town and its position required fortification against attacks from the north.

Single Combat – Goliath

There are numerous Biblical references, in texts concerned with David, to trial of battle by single combat. At the time when it was commonly believed that the 'Sea-Peoples' originated in the Aegean and Crete, parallels were drawn with the single combats to be found in the *Iliad*. Thus, it was assumed that this method of combat was introduced into Palestine from Mycenaean Greece. However, the frequency of its occurrence and further evidence for 'single combat' in non-Biblical sources does suggest it was a method of warfare both practised and understood by many in this part of the world.

The principal reason for its employment was as a simple expedient – to prevent the excessive loss of life consequent in large battles. Many armies were composed of levies called up only for the period of campaigning; and war usually began at the time of the spring equinox, after the harvest, preventing great economic dislocation in fundamentally agricultural economies. Not surprisingly, kings would try and avoid battle wherever possible so as to avoid high losses amongst the levies – basically farmers in arms and vital to the general economic well-being of the state. In other words, they were an economic resource to be very carefully husbanded and this was the motive for David preferring to employ only the professional soldiers in his wars, only calling up the militia when circumstances left him with little choice.

No single combat in the whole of history is better known than that of David and Goliath. No matter what the authenticity of the historical basis of the actual clash, it is an excellent source of understanding the rules governing single combat.

The rival armies of the Philistines and of Israel were drawn up on the hills on either side of the Valley of the Terebinth;

'And each caught his opponent by the hair, and thrust his sword into his opponent's side'. The evidence of this relief from Tell Halef is that such a form of single combat was common throughout the Eastern Mediterranean during the tenth and eleventh centuries B.C.

A champion stepped out of from the Philistine ranks; his name Goliath; he was six cubits and one span tall. On his head was a bronze helmet and he wore a breastplate of scale armour; the breastplate weighed five thousand shekels of bronze. He had bronze greaves

82

on his legs and a bronze scimitar across his shoulders. The shaft of his spear was like a weaver's beam, and the head of the spear weighed six hundred shekels of iron. A shield bearer walked in front of him.

(1 Samuel 17:4–7)

A cubit, as a unit of measurement, could vary from anything between 17 and 22 inches; the length of the forearm from the tip of the middle finger to the elbow. It follows that Goliath, even if we allow for some exaggeration in the transmission was plainly a very big man. The descriptions of other 'giants' who fought in single combat suggest that Goliath and the others all came from one family in Gath and one could interpret their excessive heights in terms of some genetic aberration. Furthermore, in an age when the rulers had champions designated to fight in single combats, their size would have marked them out for such employment. Doubtless they were taken under the 'wing' of the king, cared for, and given special treatment and training – much as for any managed prize fighter today. Goliath's weaponry and armour were plainly non-standard. As one would expect with a champion, they were not only of the best but also very valuable. The description of his sword is unusually interesting in that it is described as being of bronze rather than of the iron one would expect. Calling the sword 'a scimitar' suggests Goliath carried a very large khopesh. This may have been a matter of personal preference – the weapon looks particularly offensive

A selection of pottery recovered from major Philistine sites in Israel and dating from the twelfth or eleventh century B.C. These particular examples show the distinctive painted pattern designs employed by the Philistines.

in likely effect – or the limitations of iron technology at the time which prevented the casting of any straight sword which would have been long enough for Goliath to use. He is also described as wearing greaves and others have stressed the Aegean connection again by speaking of Goliath's armour panoply as being very similar to that worn by Greeks at the time of the Trojan wars.

The words spoken next by Goliath provide the real insight into the purpose of this type of combat:

> Why have you come out to range yourselves for battle? Am I not a Philistine and are you not Saul's lackeys? Choose a man and let him come down to me. If he can fight it out with me and kill me, we will be your servants; but if I can beat him and kill him, you become our servants and serve us!' The Philistine then said, 'I challenge the ranks of Israel today. Give me a man and we will fight it out!'

(1 Samuel 17:8–11)

Clearly Goliath was arguing that a full-scale battle is unnecessary and the whole matter could be resolved by two representative champions, one for the Philistines and the other for Israel. There would seem to have been a tacit acceptance of the idea that victory would not be disputed once the outcome of the combat was manifest. With Goliath despatched this is exactly what occurred: 'When the Philistines saw that their champion was dead, they fled'.

Details of other single combats with 'sons of Rapha' of Gath occur (2 *Samuel* 12:15ff) and they also occur in a slightly different form in 'the war between the House of Saul and the House of David' and specifically in the incident that took place at the pool of Gibeon.

The descriptions are of a ritual form of personal combat plainly understood by those involved and one that seems to have given the participants little chance of survival, whereby: 'Each caught his opponent by the head and drove his sword into his side and thus they all fell together.' The failure of the warriors to triumph over the others then requires the two opposing forces to fight it out.

Whilst such single combats seem to have occurred fairly often and may well have been a regular sight, they were never a total substitute for the full scale battles that occurred.

Campaigns and Battles

Biblical material dealing with the reign of David does not present detailed accounts of any of his battles and campaigns. Nevertheless it is possible to use what information does exist (2 *Samuel* 10:6ff and 1 *Chronicles* 19:6ff) to construct a fairly clear picture of, say, the battle fought by Joab outside of the walls of the Ammonite capital of Rabbah.

In the face of the coming Israelite attack, Hanun, King of the Ammonites, expended a thousand talents of silver to hire mercenary chariots and cavalry from the Aramaeans in Syria and the Lebanon. David heard of this arrangement and attempted to pre-empt the Aramaean forces

moving south joining up with the native Ammonite forces. The Bible text suggests that the Ammonites then deployed their forces in front of the city gates, but this would make nonsense of the claim that Joab discovered that he had to fight a battle on two fronts, unless the Ammonite army had deployed not outside of Rabbah but Heshbon. What happened there, whether at the city's gates or further south, was a testimony to the sheer professionalism of David's army and to the quick thinking of Joab. Discovering the Aramaean forces bearing down on his rear, he quickly divided his forces. In so doing, he must have had absolute faith in the ability of his men to execute the most complex of manoeuvres – to divide forces, about face and then fight a battle on two fronts. Plainly the Aramaeans were the more dangerous opponents as the best troops were deployed facing them. The other front was commanded by Joab's brother Abishai.

The battle resulted in an Israelite victory but a further campaign against the Aramaean forces by the whole of the army of Israel was required before David could claim victory in the TransJordan.

Another relief from Tell Halef, in northern Syria, showing an archer drawing back his powerful compound bow, a common but very effective weapon in the tenth century B.C.

85

The army which David created became a formidable instrument, allowing him to create an empire for the first and only time in Israel's history.

Empire

The wars which occupied the first half of David's reign as king of the united kingdom of Israel and Judah cannot be dated with any certainty. Nevertheless it is probable that they took place in the first twenty years of the tenth century B.C. The motives for this vigorous outburst of expansionism were little different from those of the Philistines or of any other power of the period bent upon conquest.

In the first instance, there was the need to establish and secure the borders of the state – which meant defeating the Philistine menace once and for all. Additionally, the successful prosecution of aggressive wars gained economic advantage for the state. Such advantage came through trade, so David was governed by the desire to control the arteries of trade that ran from Egypt through Philistia, heading northwards into Syria. To the east of Israel other trade routes also ran through the Jordan valley, originating at the northern end of the Gulf of Aqaba and ending in Damascus. At such a time of great power weakness, smaller powers such as the Philistines or Israel could partake of the 'great game', that of the control and usufruct of the goods carried on these trade routes. Under David Israel achieved glory as an imperial power as the ever present tensions between Israel and Judah were suppressed by the powerful rule of David and his successor Solomon. The centralised political structure that made the Hebrew 'empire' possible was only torn apart after their reigns were over.

That David was able to weld such a structure is testimony to the remarkable army and military organisation that developed in Israel during his reign, brought about by his own genius for organisation and charismatic leadership. It was the latter that allowed him to gather around his standard, even during the time of his rebellion against Saul, remarkable men of quality and ability. They served him all the days of his kingship with valour and unswerving loyalty. Thus, in the later days of rebellion against him, those he had least to fear were his own comrades in arms. Such then was the power base that David utilised for his achievements.

Stringed instruments based upon the lyre, with various types of percussion seem to have been prevalent (above and opposite) amongst the music of the court.

The Philistines Suppressed

The amicable relations that had existed between David and his former overlords deteriorated rapidly with his assumption of the kingship and the responsibility for protecting Israel from its enemies. David's capture of Jerusalem also provoked the Philistines to action. The strategic position of the city, astride the route of their main access to the hill country, required them to contest with David or see their whole control over the area diminish. In two actions fought in the Valley of the Rephaim – skirmish rather than battle seems the more appropriate term – the Philistines were defeated. According to the Biblical text, David then pushed them back into their own land, but of all the territories surrounding Israel, Philistia came off the best. Whilst having to reconcile themselves to the permanent loss of control over Israel, they were allowed to maintain their independence, but with vassal status. Consequently, David gained control of the trade routes running through Philistia and received a generous share in the resulting profits therefrom.

Politically, his generous treatment of the Philistines may have arisen from a desire not to provoke Egypt, although it is doubtful whether Egypt was either in a position to help or had the desire to do so. Thus, with its 'imperial' ambitions quashed and its sea trade severely constrained by the Israelites, to the very acceptable benefit of the Phoenicians, the Philistine confederation was effectively ended. Nevertheless, Philistia became an important source of mercenary soldiers for David's army and its major cities remained until the seventh century B.C. when the great imperial power of Assyria effectively absorbed them.

Aramaean Wars

It was the TransJordan territories that witnessed the hardest and bloodiest fighting of David's rule. Early in his reign, David had formed an alliance with Nahash, King of Ammon, a city state based on Rabbah and located on the site of Amman, capital of the modern state of Jordan. However, with the death of Nahash, war broke out between Israel and Ammon. Again, the most likely reason for hostilities was David's wish to acquire full control over the trade routes running through the Jordan valley. This brought about the intervention of the powerful state of Aram-Zobah, in the Bekaa valley to the northwest of Damascus, but which nevertheless viewed both Galilee and the northern TransJordan as falling within its sphere of influence. Its king, Hadadezer, was able to field powerful military forces financed principally by the rich copper mines to be found within his territories. He responded quickly to the request of Hanun, King of Ammon, who needed help in the face of a major attack on his city by the standing army of Israel under the command of Joab. Thus, with a mercenary force from Zobah and contingents from its suzerains, he hoped to defeat the Israelites. However, in a hard battle, fought on reversed fronts, Joab was able to inflict a severe defeat on his enemy, though the longer term outcome was indecisive.

Realizing that David was making a major challenge to his interests in the TransJordan region, Hadadezer raised another, larger, army. Against

them, David himself commanded not only the standing army but also the full tribal levy. At Helam, whose actual site is unknown, the two armies met in what was a major clash of arms. The biblical account (2 Samuel 10:18–19) tells how the Aramaeans drew up in line facing David and engaged in battle. David clearly proved superior as the 'Aramaeans fled from Israel'. Some 700 of their chariot teams and 40,000 men were reported killed, including Shobach, commander of the opposing army.

The consequence of this second Israelite victory was that Zobah conceded David's claim to the TransJordan and withdrew from the area. Indeed, they gave up yet more territory to Israel when David expanded northwards to embrace Galilee and acquired a border with Phoenicia. Elsewhere in the *Second Book of Samuel* it is suggested that David actually invaded Zobah, which may well have been the case, but the territory certainly did not come under direct Israelite rule.

The victories over Aram-Zobah were highly significant, for it was the most powerful kingdom in Syria and had even managed to seize territory from Assyria. Ammon, Aram-Zobah and Aram-Damascus were all required to render tribute to David as vassals of Israel.

Moab and Edom Crushed

Following in the footsteps of Saul, David also campaigned against Moab and Edom where his policy led to harsh measures being taken against the peoples of the two kingdoms.

Geographical isolation (to the south of the Wadi Mujib, known as the valley of the river Arnon in Biblical times) had meant that Moab proper rarely came under any sort of previous permanent political control by Israel. David's census of his domains, carried out by Joab and other army commanders, began at the Arnon and thus records the southward limit of Israel's harsh control over the territory.

Edom was subject to severe rule. It was an area of wild, harsh country on Israel's southern border and was garrisoned after a battle in the 'Valley of the Salt'. David's occupying forces were stationed in very uninviting conditions, with the task of ensuring border security in this part of the 'empire' and countering incursions by nomadic tribesmen from the Negev.

Dominion of Conquest

The consequence of these wars was impressive. Within twenty years of his accession to the throne of Israel, David ruled over an empire whose influence stretched from the Lebanon mountains in the north, to the borders of Egypt in the south. Ancient Israel was never again to rise to such heights. For the narrator of the *Second Book of Samuel*, and in keeping with the theological direction of the text, the great achievement lay in the recognition of God's special favour as 'David grew stronger and stronger, and Yahweh, God of Sabaoth was with him'.

The transformation of Israel into a highly centralised state was necessary in order to create the means to establish such an empire. However, this very transformation soon generated strains within the newly emerged kingdom that threatened to bring the whole structure crashing down around David's ears. The rebellions of Absalom and Sheba were the manifestation of those tensions. Within a few years of the accession of Rehoboam, son of David's successor Solomon, they were to split the land irrevocably into the kingdoms of Israel and Judah.

Troubles and Rebels

Whilst building on the foundation laid by Saul, David sought with his reign to transform the whole structure of Israel from that of a tribal society into a highly centralised state. Power was transferred from the diffuse and local level of the tribe. It was then seemingly concentrated in the hands of an individual served by a new, authoritarian and anonymous administration. This did much to alienate many in David's kingdom.

Internal Stress

There were growing social tensions too. The great influx of wealth – a consequence of success in foreign wars and more effective exploitation of existing national resources – was evident in the growing affluence of the new 'over' class in Israel. Little of this new wealth percolated down to the lower strata of society. Thus, the majority of people, whilst observing the tangible material benefits of the new order in Israel, were shut off from it. It was a situation exacerbated by a king who seemed prepared to take a humiliating and harsh census of the people. And always there existed the age-old tension between the northern and southern tribes, simmering below the surface, offering a useful and comprehensible focus for the much wider unhappiness that seemed to be emerging with a nostalgia for a return to a simpler era. Naturally, all of the above took some little while to manifest itself. Nevertheless, it seems likely that David's troubles began earlier in his reign than later. Then, at a time when there was still a great attachment in the hearts of many to his predecessor, the dead king Saul, David managed to perform an act that did much to alienate the people, and particularly the tribes of Benjamin and Ephraim.

Vengeful Execution

It would have been only prudent for David to have ensured the security of his own throne by attending to Saul's surviving male relatives. Yet he appears to have attended to their liquidation merely to satisfy the desire for blood vengeance on the part of the Gibeonites. They had pronounced

The rulers of Ammon to the east of the Jordan had many dealings with both Saul and David. Whilst David had good relations with Nahash of Ammon, shown here, he reduced his son to vassaldom.

89

a curse on all Israel for what Saul had done to them and their city. With the blood vengeance still unsatisfied at Saul's death, it devolved onto his surviving male relatives. The curse was seen to manifest itself as a three-year famine throughout Israel. To expiate Saul's guilt and end the famine, David handed over to the Gibeonites those whom they wanted:

> The king took the two sons born to Saul by Rizpah daughter of Aiah: Armoni and Meribbaal; and the five sons borne by Merab, daughter of Saul to Adriel son of Barzillai, of Meholah. He handed these over to the Gibeonites who dismembered them before Yahweh on the hill. The seven of them perished together; they were put to death in the first days of the harvest, at the beginning of the barley harvest.
>
> (2 Samuel 21:8–9)

Of course, the famine then did end.

Absalom's Rebellion

The most serious problem to face David in his reign was the rebellion of Absalom his son. Not only was David displaced from his throne for several weeks, but he very nearly lost it altogether. The basis of the rebellion lay in the ambitions of a son 'who would be king', exploiting for his own ends the many grievances that by then existed towards David's administration:

> Absalom procured a chariot and horses, with fifty men to run ahead of him. He would get up early and stand beside the road leading to the city gate; and whenever a man with some lawsuit had to come before the king's tribunal, Absalom would ask, 'Which town are you from?' If he answered, 'Your servant is from one of the tribes of Israel', then Absalom would say, 'Look your case is sound and just, but not one of the king's deputies will listen to you.' Absalom would say 'Oh, who will appoint me judge in the land? Then anyone with a lawsuit or a plea could come to me and I should see he had justice!' And whenever any one came up to him to prostrate himself, he would stretch out his hand, draw him up and kiss him. Absalom acted like this with every Israelite who appealed to the King's tribunal, and so Absalom won the Israelites' hearts.
>
> (2 Samuel 15:1–16)

A conspiracy was hatched and Absalom was crowned King at Hebron. Support for Absalom was widespread, both in the south and in the north of the kingdom, and David was forced to flee across the Jordan with the units of the standing army.

Absalom occupied Jerusalem, taking possession of his father's harem in the palace, thus declaring openly that he was now King. His failure to pursue David and defeat his father's army proved to be his undoing.

In the short time available to David, his forces were rapidly reorganised. Thus, when the clash of arms finally took place in the forest of Ephraim, Absolam's forces were routed. Ignoring the King's request to 'treat Absalom gently!' Joab killed him with three darts in his heart whilst the unlucky Absalom hung from the branches of a tree, caught up there by his long hair whilst fleeing the rout.

However, David was not automatically received back as King. Indeed, the elders of Judah and Israel may well have chosen another had not

representations on David's behalf by Zadok the priest and Abiathar led to the elders agreeing to David's reinstatement.

David's expressed willingness to retain Amasa, who had commanded Absalom's army, indicated that he would show clemency to many who had supported his son. In general, the people of Israel shortly concurred. However, recriminations between the south and north revealed the extent to which they still saw themselves as separate entities. It provided the momentum for the second rebellion to afflict David's reign.

Sheba's Revolt
Sheba, a Benjaminite, attempted to provoke a split in the kingdom and bring an end to the monarchy by raising the standard of rebellion. He appealed explicitly to the sense of identity of the northern tribes:

The Aramaeans who fought against David at Helam may well have been amongst the first peoples ever to employ cavalry. There is little or no evidence of a saddle, so the warrior probably sat on a blanket. His main weapon was a sword, and a small shield was slung over his shoulder.

We have no share in David.
we have no heritage in the son of Jesse.
Every man to his tents, O Israel!

(2 Samuel 20:1)

Although the text implies that 'all Israel' did follow Sheba, it would seem that his support was limited. Nevertheless, David reacted quickly to the threat and ordered Amasa to raise the militia of Judah within three days. Time was of the essence, so when Amasa failed to show up, David handed over the suppression of the revolt to Joab.

In pursuit of Sheba, Joab's force met Amasa marching towards them. What happened next further illustrates that Joab was not a man to be trifled with. Wearing his uniform, over which he had buckled a sword hanging from his waist in a scabbard, Joab faced the man who had displaced him as the army commander. Somehow, perhaps by deliberate design the sword fell out. Joab then said to Amasa, 'Are you well brother?' With his right hand he took Amasa by the beard in order to kiss him. Consequently, Amasa paid no attention to the sword, which Joab picked up and struck Amasa with in the belly spilling his entrails over the ground. There was no need for a second blow; Amasa lay dead.

Joab and Abishai resumed their pursuit of Sheba, running him to ground in the town of Abel Beth Maacah. Laying siege to the place proved immediately effective; the citizens decapitated Sheba and threw his head over the wall to Joab.

David had been unable to avenge himself on Amasa immediately following Absalom's rebellion because of his need to show clemency. Thus, he was perhaps as satisfied, as was Joab himself, with Amasa's death. So it was not surprising when Joab was re-instated as commander of the army rather than executed for murdering one of the King's servants.

History and Reality

In reality David's reign was not the tranquil time, nor was he the perfect ruler, that posterity portrays. As is the case of all great figures in history, the years have lessened the memory of the less pleasant aspects of personality, and of the dubious actions and questionable behaviour. Nevertheless, David's achievement was a great one and his force of personality profound. Only towards the end of his reign, with his senses failing, was anyone able to get the better of Israel's great ruler.

Dynasty

At the very end of his long reign it is apparent that David was no longer in full command of his mental faculties, a pale shadow of his former vigorous and determined self. It was thus in his dotage that the last great drama of his reign was played out, a court intrigue over the succession to the throne to which the king was seemingly oblivious. The biblical account is so obviously pro-Solomonic that his accession to the throne is presented with all the hallmarks of a palace coup. There was a split within the court, with factions supporting either Adonijah, David's eldest surviving son, or Solomon, his son by Bathsheeba. No full explanation exists for this division, but plainly mutual jealousy and ambition were powerful motivating factors.

The account in the *First Book of Kings* opens with the very enfeebled David, King in name only. A degree of power already resided with Adonijah and it seems reasonable to speculate that he also functioned as some sort of 'joint ruler' with his father, already exercising a measure of kingly authority. If that was the case, then Adonijah was quite evidently the heir designate, able to draw on the strong support of Joab (who was still commander of the army) and Abiathar the priest. Yet there must have existed a measure of ambiguity about Adonijah's position. Certainly, something allowed the pro-Solomon group to act against Adonijah and his party without being regarded as openly usurping the royal succession. The law of primogeniture may yet to have been established. Equally, perhaps David had not yet indicated who was to succeed him. Maybe he was in no position to do so because of his declining mental state. Whatever the reasons, a situation seemed to exist whereby Adonijah acted tacitly as the heir designate but that could be changed if David could be 'helped' to make a definitive choice. In all likelihood, it was an awareness on the part of the pro-Adonijah group that moves were afoot to place Solomon on the throne that led Joab and Abiathar to have Adonijah crowned even as the King still lived. Both sides were playing for very high stakes as is apparent from Nathan's words to Solomon's mother Bathsheeba on hearing the news that Adonijah had already been crowned king in a secret ceremony:

Have you not heard that unknown to our lord David, Adonijah son of Haggith has become king? Well, this is my advice to you if you want to save your own life and the life of your son Solomon.

(1 Kings 1:11–12)

Bathsheeba was then instructed to enter the king's presence and to ask him how was it that Adonijah was now king when David had already promised to make Solomon king after him. Nathan then entered a few moments later to inform the king of the news about Adonijah and to reassure David that he had made such a promise to make Solomon king. If David was indeed as addled in his thinking as the Biblical text leads us to believe, then he was unfit to dispute the claim about Solomon one way or the other. The ruse plainly worked; the royal command was given to have Solomon crowned. Solomon's supporters immediately put into operation what appears to have been a well rehearsed coup. Zadok the priest and Benaiah, commander of the palace guard, led Solomon to the place of public anointing, surrounded and escorted by the Cherethites and Pelethites. By implication the party of Solomon could ensure the loyalty of the mercenary troops who formed the palace guard.

As a result, Solomon, unlike Saul or David, was not crowned by the elders of Israel, but by a group of powerful figures in David's administration. Their action was then acclaimed by the Jerusalem crowd.

All the dealings with David went on behind the scenes, and David never seems to have endorsed Solomon publicly. One can only conclude that the whole affair was put together by a powerful clique within David's own court in order to usurp the throne from Adonijah and place Solomon there in his stead. Such a view is further supported by the actions of Solomon immediately following David's death. Adonijah was executed on a trumped up charge and Joab was killed, supposedly on the death bed orders of David, to avenge the murder of Abner so many years before and thus absolve David and his descendants of the blood guilt involved. With Joab's murder, Benaiah assumed command of the army. Abiathar was allowed to live, but his place as the king's priest was taken by Zadok.

Thus, even at the end of his days, David was surrounded by the intrigue and politics that had attended him ever since his first appearance at Saul's court. A man of driving ambition and demonic energy, he was a towering figure in the history of his people, transforming Israel from a tribal society into a centralised state equipped with the trappings consonant with monarchy in the Ancient Near East. Such were his achievements that his people were to look back on his reign as a 'Golden Age', with a nostalgia for Israel's imperial greatness, albeit transitory, that was never to be theirs again.

For nearly four hundred years, the descendants of David, son of Jesse, ruled from Jerusalem. First they ruled over all Israel and then following the division of the land into the two kingdoms, over Judah – until in 587 B.C., another great king, Nebuchadnezzar of Babylon, brought to an end forever the throne, if not the lineage, of David.

Bibliography

Anderson, B. *The Living World of the Old Testament* Longman, 1966

Bright, J. *A History of Israel* SCM 1981

Cambridge Ancient History Vol II, 2A and 2B, Cambridge University Press, 1985

Finegan, J. *Archaeological History of the Ancient Middle East* Dorset, 1986

Grant, M. *The History of Ancient Israel* Weidenfeld & Nicolson, 1986

Grant, M. *The Ancient Mediterranean* Weidenfeld & Nicolson, 1969

Heaton, E.W. *The Hebrew Kingdoms* Oxford University Press, 1968

Kenyon, K., Revised Moorey, P.R.S. *The Bible and Recent Archaeology* British Museum Publications, 1987

Miller, J.M. and Hayes, J.H. *A History of Ancient Israel and Judah* SCM, 1986

Pritchard, J.B. (ed) *The Times Atlas of the Bible* Times Books, 1987

Sandars, N.K. *The Sea Peoples* Thames and Hudson, 1985

Stillman, N. and Tallis, N. *Armies of the Ancient Near East 300 B.C.–539 B.C.* Wargames Research Group, 1984.

Yagdin, Y. *The Art of Warfare in the Biblical Lands in the Light of Archaeological Discovery* 1983

SONS BORN TO DAVID WHILST KING IN HEBRON

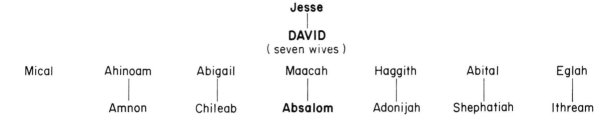

Jesse
|
DAVID
(seven wives)

Mical	Ahinoam	Abigail	Maacah	Haggith	Abital	Eglah
	Amnon	Chileab	**Absalom**	Adonijah	Shephatiah	Ithream

SONS BORN TO DAVID WHILST KING IN JERUSALEM

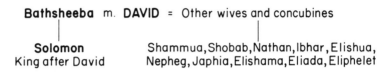

Bathsheeba m. **DAVID** = Other wives and concubines
| |
Solomon   Shammua, Shobab, Nathan, Ibhar, Elishua,
King after David   Nepheg, Japhia, Elishama, Eliada, Eliphelet

HOUSE OF SAUL
SAUL

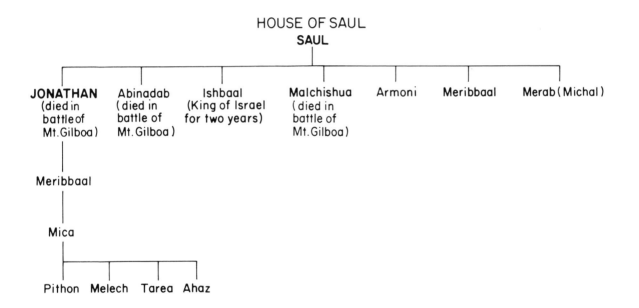

JONATHAN (died in battle of Mt. Gilboa)	Abinadab (died in battle of Mt. Gilboa)	Ishbaal (King of Israel for two years)	Malchishua (died in battle of Mt. Gilboa)	Armoni	Meribbaal	Merab (Michal)

Meribbaal
|
Mica

Pithon	Melech	Tarea	Ahaz

Nebuchadnezzar

SCOURGE OF ZION

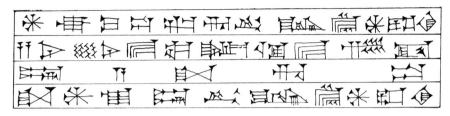

A cuneiform inscription bearing the royal stamp of Nebuchadnezzar found on mud bricks throughout Babylonia.

Nebuchadnezzar, King of Babylon
patron of Esagila and Ezida
eldest son
of Nabopolassar, King of Babylon

THE EMPIRE OF NEBUCHADNEZZAR

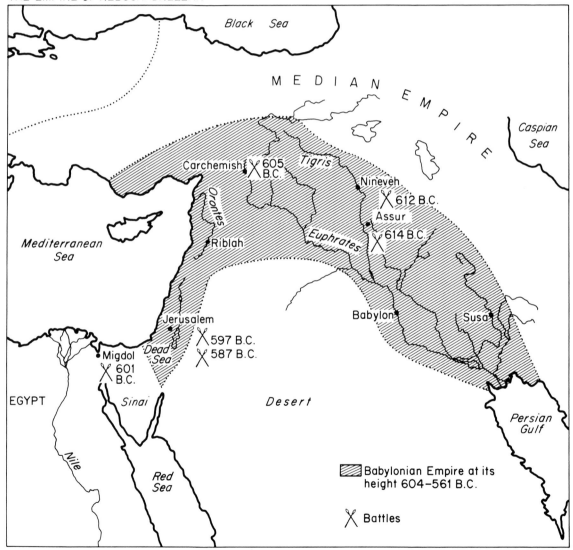

Great Babylon!
Was it not built by me as a royal residence,
By the force of my might
And for the majesty of my glory

(Daniel 4:27–28)

What Manner of Man?

There are few names from the Ancient World more illustrious than that of Nebuchadnezzar. He was a great military leader, and a brilliant tactician and strategist. However it is for the rebuilding of one great city – Babylon – and for the destruction of another – Jerusalem in 587 B.C. that he is best remembered. The consequences of the latter event and the subsequent deportation of its population into exile are still with us even though the events occurred more than twenty-five centuries ago.

Out of the despair of the destruction of Jerusalem and of the great temple built by Solomon, the Jewish exiles in Babylon forged a new vision of their faith whose influence pervades the whole of western culture through the medium of the Judeo-Christian religious tradition.

Indeed, it is from the writings of the Jewish prophets – particularly of Jeremiah, Ezekiel and Daniel – that most people are familiar with the name of Nebuchadnezzar. Whilst the verdict is generally favourable there are aspects of his character and activities that leave some seeing him in a less than favourable light. The contemporary damning of imperialism has led to some labelling him as nothing more than a godless conqueror, bent only on territorial expansion at any cost.

However, it is important that one should not judge people out of their time and impose upon their milieu, values and beliefs that would be as alien to them, as theirs would be to us. Nebuchadnezzar lived in violent and brutal times; it is sometimes easy to forget when reading of sieges and battles that appear to us to be quite horrific, that for many people the world in which we live is in reality hardly less brutal.

It is difficult at this distance in time to analyse the personality of Nebuchadnezzar in the manner that is a necessary part of modern biography. One of the more significant omissions from the reports of his activities is the bombast and vainglory with which the Assyrian kings described their military deeds. Those Babylonian inscriptions that do exist, show him to have been a pious monarch who saw his activities arising out of a warrant from the gods. This was not new or even unique

– the kings of Assyria also claimed as much. What is interesting, however, is the degree to which he saw this divine vocation in terms of the dispensation of justice:

Without you, my lord, what exists? You establish the reputation of the king whom you love, whose name you pronounce and who pleases you. You make his reputation one of justice and set a straight forward course for him. I am the prince who obeys you, the creation of your hand. You begot me and entrusted me with the rule over all peoples.

This prayer was addressed to Marduk, the principal god of Nebuchadnezzar and Babylon. Certainly, the *Book of Daniel* speaks of the King as a man anxious about matters both moral and spiritual.

Like his father, he was an undoubted imperialist and pursued a policy of territorial expansion. Both were certainly influenced by the Assyrian imperial tradition and were no doubt seen in the same light as the earlier power by those who for so long had been under their domination. It is however to his life and career that we now turn.

Son of Nabopolassar

We do not know the exact year of Nebuchadnezzar's birth but it was certainly after 630 B.C. He was the eldest son of Nabopolassar and it is he who first mentions Nebuchadnezzar when he speaks of him as helping the early repair work on the great Ziggurat of Entemenanki in Babylon in 620 B.C.

The name of Nebuchadnezzar is more correctly rendered as Nabu-kudurri-usur, from the Akkadian, meaning: 'O Nabu, protect my offspring'.

Sources for this period of his life are sparse, but of this we are certain, he was born at a time of great events in the ancient Near East. The map of the 'world' was being redrawn, the old order was passing away and new empires were emerging. Instrumental in bringing about this great change was Nabopolassar, who in helping to bring about the collapse of Assyria, laid the foundations of the Neo-Babylonian empire, which was to rise to such great heights under his son.

Nabopolassar and Babylon

Nabopolassar seized power in Babylon in the period of turmoil that followed the death in 627 B.C. of Assurbanipal, the last great King of Assyria. The empire was on the verge of civil war as a consequence of a struggle for the succession to the Assyrian throne. Nabopolassar, in the best opportunistic fashion of his Chaldean forbears, marched on Babylon and seized the kingship for himself.

As to his origins, some have ascribed to him the leadership of the

The god Marduk or Bel (Lord) was the chief deity of Babylon. The splendid temple complex of Esagila, which was restored by Nebuchadnezzar, was dedicated to Marduk.

Chaldean tribe of the Bit Yakin, and thus the kingship of the 'Sea-Lands'. Such a position would suggest the recognition of his status by the Assyrians. Nabopolassar described himself as the 'son of a nobody', which does not imply humble origins as such, but rather tells us that he was not of the recognised ruling family of Babylon. His name, correctly rendered as Nabu-apal-usur, is pure Babylonian; but it suggests his birth place was the ancient city of Borsippa to the south of Babylon, whose god, Nabu or Nebo was worshipped there. Nevertheless, his ability to seize Babylon implies a degree of status and power that allowed his usurpation of the throne to be supported and accepted by the politically powerful elements within the city itself.

Over the centuries of Assyrian domination, Babylon had erupted repeatedly in rebellion; and Chaldean involvement was nearly always the catalyst. The Assyrian response had frequently been harsh and brutal. Twice in the preceding eighty years Babylon had suffered catastrophic sieges and the damage within the city was still visible at the time of Nabopolassar's accession.

Thus, it was with the 'blessings' of the gods of the land, voiced through the powerful temple priesthood and to the acclaim of the assembled nobility and tribal chiefs, that in November 626 B.C. Nabopolassar was crowned King of Akkad (Babylon). The dynasty he inaugurated is known either as the Chaldean or Neo-Babylonian. Under the aegis of himself and his successors, Babylon was transformed into the capital of the last great Mesopotamian empire, which after a brief glory lasting less than a century passed into the hands of Cyrus the Great of Persia in 539 B.C.

Alliance for Conquest

Nabopolassar's immediate concern on achieving power was to rebuild the Babylonian army in preparation for the contest of power with Assyria. The make-up and structure of the Neo-Babylonian army are examined later, but suffice it to say at this point that it must have drawn heavily on the Assyrian model for inspiration.

On the diplomatic front Nabopolassar began the search for allies. Of these efforts the most important were the overtures he made to Cyaxares, King of the Medes of Iran, who like Babylon had a long history of domination by and tribute payment to Assyria. Furthermore the Medes had just thrown off the yoke of the Scythians who had dominated Media for some twenty-five years. According to Herodotus, Cyaxares had re-organised his army, placing it on a new footing by separating the arms into distinctive units of lancers, cavalry and archers. Cyaxares had learned well the lessons of battle taught him by the Scythians and Assyrians and was now ready to turn this very formidable instrument of war against Nineveh itself, capital of Assyria. In the light of the subsequent role played by the Median armies against Assyria, it was their

An Akkadian infantryman of the Babylonian royal guard. Such soldiers attended Nebuchadnezzar when on campaign. Their uniform and equipment draw heavily on Assyrian types and designs.

participation that was in all likelihood the determining factor in Assyria's ultimate defeat. Although not formally bound by treaty, there is evidence to suggest that Babylon and Media began to act in concert on military operations directed at Assyria as early as 621 B.C.

Nabopolassar felt strong enough to first take the field against Assyria in 616. However, the next two years witnessed an indecisive march and countermarch by the rival armies as they jostled for advantage, their operations focussing on a line of Assyrian fortresses straddling the northern border of Babylonia.

It was at this time that a small Egyptian force made its appearance fighting alongside the Assyrians, heralding the appearance of yet another player in the drama that was unfolding on the Euphrates. This was only a token Egyptian force, but presaged the much greater involvement of this power in a conflict whose outcome was of great significance for her long-term interests in northern Syria and the lands of the Mediterranean seaboard.

The impasse was broken in 614 when Cyaxares invaded the heartland of Assyria itself. He had the intention of taking the imperial capital, but its massive defences defied the besiegers. Turning south, the fury of the Medes fell upon the city of Assur and in the words of the *Babylonian Chronicle*:

He (the Mede), says our Chronicle, made an attack upon the town . . . and the city wall he destroyed. He inflicted a terrible massacre upon the greater part of the people, plundering it and carrying off prisoners from it.

Nabopolassar and his army arrived too late to take part in the sack of the city, but amidst the smoking ruins of the former capital of the Empire, he and Cyaxares 'established mutual friendship and peace' and concluded the alliance that sealed the fate of the Assyrian Empire.

In personal terms, the most important outcome of the alliance between Babylon and Media was the marriage between Nebuchadnezzar and Amytis, the daughter of Cyaxares. Tradition relates that it was for her that he built that wonder of the Ancient World, the Hanging Gardens.

School of War

The storm god Adad worshipped by both Assyrians and Babylonians. The western gate in the 'new' city of Babylon was named for Adad.

It seems reasonable to suppose that as he was growing to manhood, Nebuchadnezzar accompanied his father on his campaigns, observing at first hand the complexities of the art of war. The close co-operation that ensued between the Babylonian and Median armies would have exposed the young man to the different methods employed by the respective armies. The abilities he showed later on the battlefield must have their origin in this period. Certainly, the great events unfolding around him could scarcely have provided a more suitable training for a future reign that was spent almost annually in the field.

Thus, his military career began whilst he was still a young man, and he was appointed to his first command in the year 610 B.C. As a military administrator in Babylonia, he raised troops to send to his father who was campaigning in the Harran area. The very fact that he was not with his father suggests that he was deemed responsible enough by Nabopolassar to deputise for the King in his absence. Although we cannot be certain of his age at this time, his preparation for his military responsibilities began many years before.

From an early age Nebuchadnezzar would have been conscious of the impact of war on Babylon. Virtually every year he would have watched his father, in his chariot, lead out the army through the Ishtar Gate to campaign in the north against the Assyrians. At court, which was constantly full of high ranking officers, he would overhear conversations of the battles fought on the frontier – and no doubt in deference to his status some of these soldiers would tell him of their experiences and relate anecdotes of life in the field.

As he grew older he began his own military training under the skilful eye of veterans appointed by his father. They would have developed his expertise with the sword, lance and bow. Others would have trained him in horsemanship and in the difficult and dangerous task of controlling a chariot team. As he matured, his training would have been expanded to cover such matters as strategy and tactics, siege warfare and logistics. He would have become acquainted with the different units that made up the Babylonian army, learning to understand their strengths and weaknesses. As the war against Assyria entered its final phase it seems likely that his father would have included him in any discussions in which political and military strategy were discussed with his senior officers. Very probably he joined his father on campaign, as was suggested earlier, and was in all likelihood present at the fall of Assur and

Chaldean infantry like these provided the bulk of the troops fielded by the Babylonian armies. Their body protection was minimal and they were lightly armed, with the compound bow their main weapon. Spears and wicker shields enabled these soldiers to close in upon their enemy.

Nineveh. His marriage to Cyaxares' daughter Amytis laid the foundation of the initially good relationship that existed between Media and himself when he was King. His first-hand observations of the Median armies in action must have had some effect on his handling of Babylonian troops who under his father were never noted for their military prowess. The very fact that Nebuchadnezzar, within a few short months of being appointed its commander-in-chief, could take the Babylonian army and destroy the Egyptian army suggests that he possessed a remarkable military talent.

In 607–606, having been designated Crown Prince, he commanded an army with his father in northern Assyria. Nabopolassar returned to Babylon after a month and left the young Crown Prince in charge of the army. He undertook independent operations against rebellious hill tribesmen, a campaign of four months, which culminated in the destruction and looting of a city. Thereafter he was constantly engaged in military operations to help his father. By 605 B.C., the Babylonian monarch's declining health and the growing proof of Nebuchadnezzar's military abilities led to Nabopolassar handing over the army to his son. With that army Nebuchadnezzar was to create in less than twenty years an empire that at its height was larger than that of Assyria under Assurbanipal. Clearly, in the hands of Nebuchadnezzar it became a formidable instrument of power and is deserving of a closer study.

Forces of Battle

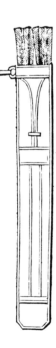

Whilst no Babylonian counterpart exists of the wall reliefs from the palaces of the Assyrian kings, it is likely the Neo-Babylonian armies of Nebuchadnezzar drew heavily on the organisation, types of equipment and tactics employed by the Assyrian army at the time of Assurbanipal. Also, the Babylonians had contact with the armies of Elam, often in alliance with them against Assyria, and affecting the tactics and make-up of aspects of the Neo-Babylonian forces. Additionally, Nebuchadnezzar's own observations and experience of Median military methods had some influence on the way his forces evolved.

The Babylonian Army
The Babylonian army of Nebuchadnezzar was almost certainly composed of two principal elements. The core of the fighting force was made up of professional soldiers who provided the royal guard, the chariotry, the heavy cavalry and the engineer troops.

Whilst most of the soldiers were native Babylonians (Akkadian), Nebuchadnezzar certainly made use of Greek mercenary troops, but not on the scale of his Egyptian opponents. Elite units were also drawn from the Chaldean tribes of the 'Sea-Lands' and it is entirely conceivable that soldiers from the tribe of the Bit Yakin formed part of the King's personal bodyguard. Such then were the units that made up the standing army and which were available for garrison duties in the empire.

In the campaigning season the standing army was joined by the second component, tribal levies called to the 'colours' by the King. Most of these troops were Chaldean and were organised in tribal units. Unlike the units of the standing army they were very lightly equipped and in battle provided the bulk of the forces. Whilst they were important, it was on the units of the standing army that Nebuchadnezzar depended to gain victory. It is significant that in the one 'detailed' reference to a major battle in the *Babylonian Chronicle*, that at Migdol in 601 B.C., it was the very heavy losses amongst the cavalry and chariotry that brought about a Babylonian withdrawal from Egypt. Without those elements of the army, it was impossible for Nebuchadnezzar to bring a decisive end to the campaign.

Battlefield Tactics

In the light of observations of the make-up of the Babylonian army, the line-up on the field of battle would look as follows:

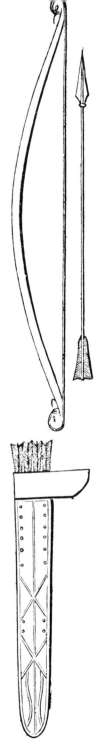

HEAVY CHARIOTS	CHALDEAN LEVIES Mass archers with light infantry armed with spears / shields	HEAVY CHARIOTS
CAVALRY		CAVALRY

	ROYAL GUARD More heavily armoured infantry	

	KING (?)	

At the beginning of the battle, long-range fire would be opened on the enemy lines by the massed archers of the tribal levies. It is possible that this fire might have been sustained for some considerable time until the King or the commanding officer perceived some wavering in the enemy lines. It would have been directed at the foot soldiers, but more particularly at the enemy's chariot forces and cavalry. At a given signal, the heavy four-horsed chariots would begin their charge, the archer(s) on board firing on the move. Shield bearers on the chariots would attempt

Amongst many quivers used with bows by the Babylonian army (above and opposite), many would have shown the strong influence of Assyrian design.

105

A heavy, four-horsed chariot similar to the type employed by the Babylonians as the main shock weapon in their battles. Although this is a late Assyrian model, from the reign of Assur-banipal, Babylonian chariots looked little different.

to protect the chariot crew from the enemy counter-fire. The effect of the chariot was both physical (little could stop such a heavy vehicle at full tilt and any infantry caught in its path would be run down) and psychological (the sight of charging massed chariots unnerving the enemy and causing them to flee in panic).

The cavalry would then follow up to exploit the gaps created in the enemy lines, and if possible turn the flanks in an encircling movement. If the enemy began a full-scale retreat, then their task was to harry, pursue and ride down the escaping soldiers.

Once the chariots and cavalry were engaged the central infantry would advance and close with the opposition. A large number of the light troops were equipped with spears, swords and large wicker shields to enable them to engage in close combat.

Such a battle would soon become a very bloody mêlée with little quarter being given by either side. Some sense of the sheer ferocity of the ancient battlefield can be gained by considering a report by the Assyrian king Sennacherib when he fought against a combined Elamite and Chaldean-Babylonian army in 691 B.C.:

I rushed upon the enemy like the approach of a hurricane . . . I put them to rout and turned them back. I transfixed the troops of the enemy with javelins and arrows. Humban undasha, the commander-in-chief of the King of Elam, together with his nobles . . . I cut their throats like sheep . . . My prancing steeds, trained to harness, plunged into their welling blood as into a river; the wheels of my battle chariot were bespattered with blood and filth. I filled the plain with the corpses of their warriors like herbage . . . There were chariots with their horses, whose riders had been slain as they came into the fierce battle, so that they were loose by themselves; those horses kept going back and forth all over the place to a distance of two double hours . . . As to the sheikhs of the Chaldeans, panic from my onslaught overwhelmed them like a demon. They abandoned their tents and fled for their lives, crushing the corpses of their troops as they went . . . In their terror they passed scalding urine and voided their excrement into their chariots.

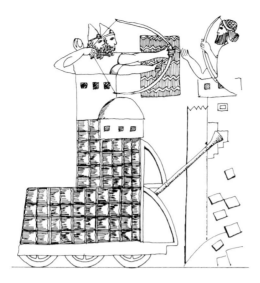

Mobile siege towers with battering rams were used in the taking of cities. Though no actual depiction of the Babylonian siege machines survived, their use and size must have been similar to those of Assurbanipal's army.

A very large siege tower (with inset of archer to show scale) from the ninth century B.C. The Babylonian forces drew heavily upon Assyrian siege experience.

Siege Warfare

Throughout the reign of Nebuchadnezzar the Babylonian army was required to undertake a large number of sieges.

Siege warfare was the most complex of operations for an army to undertake in ancient times. Certainly the Babylonian army was provided with a siege train which accompanied the advance of the main army when on campaign. As in the case of the Assyrian examples, much of the material to build the siege towers would have been carried on wagons in parts broken down for re-assembly where needed, although there are a number of texts that also imply that the fully assembled siege towers were actually manhandled across considerable distances ready for use. The *Babylonian Chronicle* refers to a campaign in 603-602 B.C., the second year of Nebuchadnezzar's reign, to some point in the west which is assumed to refer to Hatti-Land in which a town (city) was laid siege to by bringing the siege towers across the mountains.

Whilst the major powers could contest with each other on the battlefield, smaller powers such as Judah, did not have the resources to field large armies to stave off predatory imperial powers. Consequently, they applied themselves to creating highly effective defences around their major cities that would frustrate, and hopefully defeat, the attempts of besieging forces to conquer them. As defences became more effective, the main strategy for taking a fortified city was to allow starvation and disease to take its toll on the people within the walls. Earthworks would be thrown up around the city to enclose the populace and the besieging army would then wait until the moment was deemed appropriate to finally storm the walls at their weakest point.

A number of sources speak of the Babylonian armies bringing large siege towers into action. Alas, we have no direct renderings of these engines although it is extremely likely that they were very similar to the

107

larger Assyrian types. The use of these siege towers would have covered the operations of battering rams and mining operations designed to breach the walls. The problems of siege warfare can be gauged by the time taken to capture Jerusalem and the Phoenician city of Tyre. Jerusalem was under siege for two years, whereas Tyre tied down Babylonian troops for some thirteen years. (Although it has to be said that Tyre raised particular problems, being very difficult to invest properly by virtue of its isolation from the mainland; and a sheltered harbour allowed it to be supplied by vessels of its own fleet and that of Egypt.)

The Egyptian Army

In many ways the Egyptian army fielded by Necho II at Carchemish operated in a manner almost identical to that of the Babylonian forces opposing them. The traditional, central disposition of infantry with the chariots on the wings supported by cavalry would have led to tactics very similar to those of the Babylonians. However, the power of the Babylonian chariotry may well have been greater by virtue of the larger size of the chariot and crew, with a correspondingly greater effectiveness in the charge. A further difference is that the Egyptian infantry were far better organised for close order fighting than were those of Babylon, with fewer archers.

The impact of the heavily armoured and armed *haw-nebu* or 'new foreigner' from Asia Minor had a profound effect on the Egyptian army in the Saite period. The presence of these Greek mercenaries at Carchemish has been confirmed by the discovery by archaeologists of a Greek greave and bronze shield with a gorgon's head, amidst the arrow-riddled remains of a building containing a number of Egyptian items, some bearing the cartouche of Necho II. Other Greek mercenaries served with the Judaean army; evidence of their presence has been found at Mesad Hashavyahu, thought to have been a Greek mercenary settlement.

Nebuchadnezzar's chariots carried a crew of four. Two shield bearers provided cover for the driver and archer. Thus, the chariot could be used as a fighting platform, advancing and withdrawing from enemy lines.

108

The Fall of Nineveh

Two years after Nebuchadnezzar's marriage, a combined Babylonian and Median army attacked Nineveh itself. The *Babylonian Chronicle* describes the final demise of the great city:

From the month of Sivan to the month of Ab three battles were fought. They made a strong attack on the citadel and in the month of Ab the city was taken and a great defeat inflicted on the people and their chiefs. On that same day Sin-shar-ishkun, the Assyrian king, perished in the flames. They carried off much spoil from the city and temple area and turned the city into a ruin mound and heap of debris.

The speed with which the city fell is surprising, lending credence to traditions found in Greek and Biblical sources that an entrance into the city was effected by diverting the waters of a river, probably the Khosr, against the walls. These then washed away some of the city's powerful defences.

For nearly three hundred years Assyria had dominated the Fertile Crescent, its seemingly invincible armies ranging in their incessant campaigns from Elam and the Persian Gulf in the east to Egypt in the west. The great cities of Assyria had grown fabulously wealthy from the booty and tribute from the lands over which she held sway. Few had escaped their power and their record of cruelty had endeared them to none. Thus, with Nineveh's destruction, there were none to mourn Assyria's passing.

One of the very few depictions of the soldiers available to us from the Neo-Babylonian period. Detail is sparse, but the soldier on the left of the middle frame is clearly employing a compound bow, one of the major weapons of the troops in Nebuchadnezzar's army.

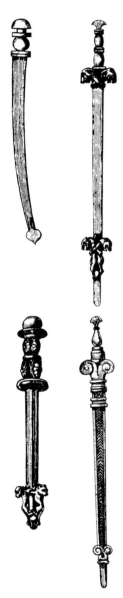

These ornately wrought iron swords were first worn by Assyrian officers, and later by the high ranking members of Nebuchadnezzar's army, who took pride in such finely worked iron weaponry.

The significance of the event was not lost on Nabopolassar. In the sweetness of victory, he contemplated the final triumph of Babylon over Nineveh:

I slaughtered the land of Subarum (Assyria), I turned the hostile land into heaps and ruins. The Assyrian, who since distant days had ruled over all peoples, and with his heavy yoke had brought injury to the people of the Land, his feet from Akkad I turned back, his yoke I threw off.

The rump of the Assyrian army retreated westwards to the city of Harran to await the arrival of assistance from their Egyptian allies. Thus, it was in Harran that one Assur-uballit, a junior member of the royal family, was crowned as the last King of Assyria.

As the pitiful remnants of the Assyrian army posed no further threat, the victorious allies parted. Cyaxares returned to his homeland, his army weighed down with booty and prisoners by the thousands destined for the slave markets of Media. Nabopolassar, intent on exploiting the collapse of Assyrian power, moved quickly to occupy as many of their former lands as he could.

Battle of Harran and Aftermath

The next two years were spent in the lands of the middle Euphrates in operations designed to enforce Babylonian control on an area that had for centuries been part of Assyria. It was a two-year breathing space that allowed Assur-uballit in Harran to regroup his forces and bolster his army with reinforcements from Egypt.

In 610 the Medes and the Babylonians moved against Harran. In the face of overwhelmingly superior forces:

Assur-uballit and the army of Egypt which had come to help him, the fear of the enemy fell on them, they abandoned the city and crossed the river Euphrates. The Babylonian king reached Harran . . . captured the city they carried off much spoil from the city and temple.

The Medes withdrew – once again satisfied with the booty from the sacked city as the price of their exertions – to establish their own empire in Armenia and Asia Minor. The sack and occupation of Harran placed the Babylonian forces in a strong position. As they were poised to advance into Syria, a land long coveted by the great powers of the Fertile Crescent for its strategic position and its great economic wealth, other forces were about to enter the game.

Carchemish and Coronation

It was the news of the defeat at Harran that prompted the new Pharaoh of Egypt, Necho II (610–595 B.C.) to call out the whole of his army and march northwards to support the remnants of Assur-uballit's forces.

Necho successfully effected a junction with the forces of the Assyrian King at Carchemish, but not before defeating the army of Josiah, King of Judah at Megiddo. The motives of Josiah in seeking battle with the Egyptians are unclear. Certainly, the very brief account does little to enlighten us:

Pharaoh Necho king of Egypt was advancing to meet the king of Assyria at the river Euphrates, and king Josiah went to intercept him; but Necho killed him at Megiddo in the first encounter.

(2 Kings 24:29)

Amidst the possible answers that have been offered, a most credible explanation lies in a diplomatic overture by Nabopolassar to Josiah, with some political inducement for him to take the field and attempt to bar the passage of the Egyptian army. Nevertheless, Megiddo was but a diversion. The main task of what was an overwhelming Egyptian army in northern Syria was to block the Babylonian drive towards the Mediterranean.

End of Empire

The initial success could not be sustained and the force withdrew to Carchemish. The name of Assur-uballit disappears hereafter from the *Chronicle* and with his demise the last traces of the Assyrian empire disappeared forever. With their ally finally destroyed, the Egyptian effort lay subsequently in the defeat of a major Babylonian offensive which was designed to take the rest of Syria, and with its fall the whole of the Mediterranean seaboard including Palestine.

Such a task seemed at first possible. The three years following the second battle of Harran saw a jostling for military advantage by both armies, with neither gaining the upper hand. It was the appointment of the Crown Prince, Nebuchadnezzar, to the command of the army in Syria in 605 B.C. that ended the stalemate. Within a few short months he had shattered the Egyptian army in a battle so decisive that according to the Bible:

The king of Egypt did not leave his own country again, because the king of Babylon had conquered everywhere belonging to the king of Egypt from the Torrent of Egypt to the river Euphrates.

(2 Kings 24:7)

The apprenticeship in arms of the young Nebuchadnezzar provides considerable insight into the truly decisive nature of the battle. Whilst the armies themselves were important it was the qualitative difference brought to the battlefield by the generalship of Nebuchadnezzar himself that was the deciding factor.

Victory

The battle of Carchemish can truly be described as one of the decisive battles of the Ancient World. Yet as with many other specific incidents

As for the remnant of the Egyptian army which had escaped from the defeat so hastily that no weapon touched them, the Babylonian army overwhelmed them and defeated them in the district of Hamath, so that not a single man escaped to his own country.

The consequence of the battle was quite clear:

At that time Nebuchadnezzar conquered the whole land of Hatti.

Nebuchadnezzar was probably at Riblah, which was to become the main Babylonian garrison in southern Syria and the base for his future operations in the west, when the news of his father's death reached him:

For twenty one years Nabopolassar had been king of Babylonia. On the eighth of Ab he died; in the month of Elul Nebuchadnezzar returned to Babylon.

According to Berosus, the third century Babylonian priest and historian:

the prisoners . . . Jews, Phoenicians, Syrians and those of Egyptian nationality were consigned to some of Nebuchadnezzar's friends, with orders to conduct them to Babylonia along with the heavy troops and the rest of the spoils; while he himself, with a small escort, pushed across the desert to Babylon.

Nebuchadnezzar reached Babylon and on 'the first day of Elul' – 6th September 605 B.C. – he sat on the royal throne that he was to occupy for forty-two years. There were no problems in the city and the accession passed smoothly to him.

At the beginning of his accession year he celebrated the New Year Festival in Babylon. The high point of the celebration occurred when the King had 'taken the hand of Bel Marduk and the son of Bel to lead them

A view of Babylon's remains from the north of the famous Procession Street, clearly showing the reconstruction work being undertaken by the Iraqi Department of Antiquities. This 'street' stretched from the Ishtar Gate to the middle of the city, and along it, at the time of the New Year Festival, would have passed the images of Marduk and the other gods on their way to the Akitu House, beyond the inner city walls. The Festival was a significant event in the city's religious calendar.

In November 598 B.C. Nebuchadnezzar mustered his army and led them forth through the Ishtar Gate Babylon to campaign in the 'Hatti' land – a familiar event – and to chastise the rebel Judah.

out in the procession'. For Nebuchadnezzar, the event was of immense significance for it was from the hand of Marduk – 'his lord' – that the new King claimed the grant of universal kingship along with the request petitioned in prayer that he: 'have no opponent from horizon to sky'.

Prophets and Kings

It is a measure of Nebuchadnezzar's authority in Babylon itself that within a very short time of his coronation he returned to Syria–Lebanon. From his base of operations at Riblah he directed his armies in a wide-ranging campaign designed to pacify the area and bring it to heel:

In the accession year Nebuchadnezzar went back to Hatti-land and marched victoriously through it until the month of Sebat. In the month of Sebat he took the heavy tribute of the Hatti-land back to Babylon.

Riches of Conquest

For nearly two millennia the lands of Syria and the Lebanon had witnessed the tramp of foreign soldiers as in their turn Egyptian, Hittite, Assyrian and now Babylonian armies sought to control the immense mineral and commercial wealth of the area to their own advantage. From the mountains of the Lebanon came the mighty cedars and cypresses whose trunks were used by many of the monarchs of the Fertile Crescent to adorn their palaces and temples. Indeed, Nebuchadnezzar tells us in great detail (in an inscription cut into a rock face in the valley of Brissa) of a campaign directed towards securing access to and control of the cedars of the Lebanon:

Judaean spearman with a typical heavy leather shield, strengthened with bronze around the rim and boss. Although the soldier shown here was in the service of the Assyrian King Sennacherib, Judean troops at the time of Nebuchadnezzar would have looked little different.

At that time Mount Lebanon, the (cedar) mountain, luxuriant forest of Marduk, sweet scented . . . over which an enemy alien held sway and was taking away its produce. Its population were scattered and had taken refuge in distant places. In the strength of Nabu and Marduk my lords, I drew up (my troops) in an array for battle against Lebanon to (take it). I cleared out its enemy on the heights and in the lowlands I made glad the hearts of the land. I gathered together its scattered population and brought them back to their place. A thing which no former king had done (that is) I broke up the towering mountains, I ground the limestone, and thus I opened up approaches and made a straight way for the cedars. I made the Arakhtu canal carry as though they were reeds, the hardy, tall, stout cedars, of surpassing quality and impressively black of aspect, solid products of mount Lebanon, to Marduk my king.

Other produce of the mountains included gold, silver, copper and precious stones. Into Tyre and Sidon, the great ports of Phoenicia, flowed the 'yield of the sea', for the commerce of the Mediterranean lands had for many centuries been brought into the near east in Phoenician vessels. Many of the luxury goods on which the Assyrians had depended, and which the Babylonians now wished for themselves, came from these Levantine ports. The goods and the taxes levied upon them now belonged to Nebuchadnezzar by right of conquest.

The economic importance of the area was further enhanced by virtue of it being the confluence of a number of vital trade routes. Of these, the most important were those from the south, whose passage through Palestine made their dislocation unacceptable to the Babylonians. Whilst Egyptian interests in the area, which were almost identical to those of Babylon, had received a reversal at the battle of Carchemish, her continued ambitions in Syria–Lebanon resulted in efforts to stir up trouble in areas now under Babylonian domination. Neither Phoenicia, Philistia nor Judah, who had for many decades each been vassals of Assyria, had any desire to pay tribute to another Mesopotamian power so soon after the fall of Nineveh, an event which had raised their hopes of freedom and independence.

Struggle in Judah

In the year following his coronation, Nebuchadnezzar marched unopposed into Palestine. Following the Babylonian siege of the Philistine city of Ashkelon, Jehoiakim, King of Judah submitted to Nebuchadnezzar and became his vassal. The tribute levied on Judah included articles and vessels from the great temple in Jerusalem and according to the *Book of Daniel*: 'These he took away to Shinar (Babylon), putting the vessels into the treasury of his own gods'.

The seeming invincibility of the arms of the Babylonian monarch had thus temporarily forced the people of Judah to reconcile themselves to paying tribute to the new Mesopotamian power. It was a bitter pill to have to swallow.

Such was the backdrop against which a dramatic confrontation was taking place in Judah itself. At stake was the continued survival of the throne of David and at issue was the way Judah should conduct itself in the face of the changed international situation. The struggle is personified in the perspectives of the two principal antagonists, whose perspectives deserve examination if one is to understand the significance of the subsequent events.

Who Speaks for Yahweh?

When in 609 B.C. the body of the thirty-nine year old Josiah was returned to Jerusalem for burial, his younger son Jehoahaz was chosen to succeed him. However, the wishes of the people of Judah did not accord with those of the Pharaoh of Egypt. Upon presenting himself to Necho II at Riblah, to acknowledge the Egyptian as Judah's overlord, the Pharaoh had him placed in chains and deprived Jehoahaz of his crown.

This act was sufficient to show that Judah was still the vassal of the Pharaoh of Egypt and that in appointing a king for themselves, the people of Judah had presumed for themselves a right that remained a preserve of their overlord. The new King, Jehoiakim, together with the majority of the political establishment of Judah, remained loyal to

Judean archers, at the time of Nebuchadnezzar's invasion would have been equipped very similarly to this earlier archer from Judah, a captive in the service of Sennacherib, the Assyrian king.

115

Egypt. It was only when the reality of Babylonian power was made manifest with the destruction of Ashkelon that Jehoiakim reluctantly transferred his loyalty to Nebuchadnezzar. The King of Judah paid tribute to Nebuchadnezzar for only three years before openly rebelling against his Babylonian overlord. That in itself is testimony that his submission was but an expedient, pending what he and many others in Judah believed to be the imminent and inevitable resurgence of the fortunes of Egypt in Palestine.

Optimism for the future of Judah, under the benevolent hegemony of the great southern power, was in marked contrast to the message of one Jeremiah, son of Hilkiah, a prophet of Yahweh, the God of the Jews, who had already pronounced the sentence of doom on the whole nation:

> So . . . this is what Yahweh Sabaoth says, 'Since you have not listened to my words, I shall send for all the families of the north (Yahweh declares, that is for Nebuchadnezzar king of Babylon, my servant) and bring them down on this country and its inhabitants (and on all the surrounding nations); I shall curse them with utter destruction and make them an object of horror, of scorn, and ruin them for ever. From them I shall banish the shouts of rejoicing and mirth, the voices of bridegroom and bride, the sound of the handmill and the light of the lamp; and this whole country will be reduced to ruin and desolation, and these nations will be enslaved to the king of Babylon for seventy years.'
>
> (Jeremiah 25:8–12)

Such, in essence, was the message read to the Temple priesthood by Baruch, a scribe employed by Jeremiah, as the prophet himself was banned from preaching within the Temple precincts. It is not surprising that the message generated alarm, and to many listening sounded like treason. Consequently, Baruch and his master were advised to go into hiding, while the scroll itself was taken before the King and read to him.

A temple official by the name of Jehudi had been ordered by the King to appear before him and read the text of Jeremiah's scroll. The winter that year was undoubtedly cold, for Jehoiakim was warming himself within the palace in front of a blazing brazier when Jehudi arrived. What follows gives us an insight into the personality of Jehoiakim:

> Each time Jehudi had read three or four columns, the king cut them off with a scribe's knife and threw them into the fire in the brazier until the whole scroll had been burnt in the brazier fire. But in spite of hearing all these words, neither king nor any of the courtiers took alarm or tore their clothes, and although Elnathan and Delaiah and Gemariah had urged the king not to burn the scroll he would not listen to them.
>
> (Jeremiah 36:23–26)

As the temple officials had feared, Jehoiakim ordered the arrest of Jeremiah. But he and Baruch could not be found and upon hearing of the destruction of the first scroll, Jeremiah had dictated another. Nothing illustrates the depth of the antipathy that existed between the two men better than Jehoiakim's treatment of the scroll. Clearly, in his calm and deliberated dismissal he regarded its contents as the rantings of a madman. The prophets had always had uncertain relationships with the kings whom they addressed, but Jehoiakim's destruction of the scroll shows the degree to which he believed the words of Jeremiah to be an utter irrelevancy to Judah's situation.

In his new scroll, Jeremiah revealed the depth of his loathing for the man who occupied the throne of David. He saw in Jehoiakim's dismissal of the contents of the scroll – the word of Yahweh – evidence of the very sin of arrogance which would doom Judah.

A Chosen People

At the heart of the Jewish tradition – thereafter inherited and developed by Christianity in a modified and distinct manner – is a conviction that there exists a special relationship between the Jews and the one true God. Specifically, it is an article of the Jewish faith that in about the thirteenth century B.C. their ancestors were liberated from slavery in Egypt. The significance of the Exodus from Egypt lay in the conviction that Yahweh had intervened decisively in history in order to bring about an event that could not have occurred if left to human devices.

In the desert of the Sinai, a more formal relationship was established between Yahweh and the Hebrew tribes when they freely entered into a legal and binding agreement called a covenant. The terms of the covenant, as communicated through Moses, required that the Hebrew tribes agreed to live by Yahweh's commandments. In return, they would be given a land of their own. As long as the Commandments of Yahweh were upheld, then Yahweh would ensure that his bounty and beneficence were enjoyed by his chosen people; but in the event of the people forsaking their obligations under the covenant, He would punish them.

The task laid upon the prophets throughout the period of the Hebrew kingdoms was to speak out for Yahweh in the face of the people's breaking of the Commandments. Always their denunciation of the backsliding of the chosen people ended with a promise of Yahweh's punishment in a manner that saw the emergence of a very different explanation of historical events. Yahweh, as the one true God, was also the Lord of history and thus able to call on the nations of all lands to effect his purpose. To the prophets, there was a rationale to international affairs that transcended the mundane explanation of events as being the mere product of the policies of the great powers.

Thus, the mighty nations of the ancient near east became the unwitting pawns whereby Yahweh punished his chosen people. The prophet Isaiah had seen even Assyrian imperialism as part of the divine purpose; other prophets of Judah saw in the armies of Babylon and in the person of Nebuchadnezzar the latest instrument of Yahweh's wrath against his people.

Therefore, Jeremiah became the most prominent voice against those who put their trust in Egypt. For him, the submission of Judah to Babylon was inevitable, for Nebuchadnezzar was the chosen instrument of Yahweh. So, to entertain escape from the domination of the Mesopotamian monarch was inviting the destruction that he had already foreseen as inevitable. Indeed, Jeremiah poured scorn on those who naively believed that Yahweh would not countenance the destruction of Jerusalem simply because the great temple built by Solomon was located there.

Jehoiakim ignored the words of Jeremiah and having paid tribute to Nebuchadnezzar for only three years, in 600 B.C. he actually withheld payment to his overlord. That made him legally in breach of his submission to the King of Babylon, and technically in a state of rebellion against Nebuchadnezzar. Such an action was bound to bring forth a harsh military response.

What could possibly have motivated such an irresponsible and potentially suicidal action? The answer lies outside of Judah itself, on the wider stage of the confrontation between Babylon and Egypt.

War with Egypt

In the fourth year of his reign, Nebuchadnezzar called up his army and, as in previous years, marched to 'the Hatti-land'. His task was to replenish the military garrisons with new troops and supplies, and generally oversee the security situation on the southern border with Egypt.

From his forward base at Riblah, the main Babylonian garrison in southern Syria, he held court. It was to Riblah that his vassals travelled with their annual tributes, continuing tokens of their submission to him. However, it was not only gold, silver and other valuables that he demanded from them. Military intelligence of Egyptian intentions in southern Palestine was vital to the Babylonian capacity to maintain control of the area. Thus, Nebuchadnezzar had charged each vassal, including Jehoiakim, in his loyalty oath to 'keep the country for him and attempt no uprising nor show friendliness to the Egyptians'. No doubt part of this requirement was to forward to the military commanders in Syria any intelligence of Egyptian actions and intentions in the area. One must also presume that, like the Assyrians, Nebuchadnezzar had a well-developed system of spies reporting regularly. Collation of these reports would thus have allowed him to keep his eye on the Egyptians and on his vassals as well.

In addition, Nebuchadnezzar most likely anticipated trouble in the area. Given that Jehoiakim was a protégé of Necho II, and had been dealt with harshly as a consequence by Nebuchadnezzar in 604 B.C., the Babylonians more than half expected the Judaean monarch to rebel if the situation in Palestine should turn in Egypt's favour. The desire to maintain control in southern Palestine, and to ensure the loyalty of his vassals in the area, meant that Nebuchadnezzar would have to take rapid

Archers of Nebuchadnezzar's time stringing their powerful compound bows and checking their arrows for alignment prior to battle. This depiction is based upon an Assyrian wall relief of the period.

and decisive action in the face of Egyptian attempts to destabilize the area.

Whether this was perceived to be precisely the case by the Babylonian King late in 601 B.C. is uncertain. Nevertheless, after raising his army to full strength – which possibly included calling upon the soldiers of his vassals, including a very reluctant Jehoiakim – Nebuchadnezzar marched south to begin a major military operation interpreted by some commentators as a full-scale invasion of Egypt.

Victory at Migdol

Nebuchadnezzar may well have concluded that an invasion of Egypt was the only solution that in the longer term would keep Palestine secure. Whatever his motivation, his invasion resulted in the largest and bloodiest battle since Carchemish.

Identifying the exact site of this battle is problematic. Some authorities speak of the Gaza plain. Alternatively, Herodotus of Halicarnassus, the Greek historian, speaks of King Necos (Necho II) attacking the Syrians (Babylonians) by land and defeating them at Magdolus (or Migdol), which is in Egypt itself on the eastern edge of the Nile delta and identified as the site of Tell el-Heir. In the words of the *Babylonian Chronicle*:

In the month of Kislev he took the lead of his army and marched toward Egypt. The king of Egypt heard of it and sent out his army; they clashed in an open battle and inflicted heavy losses on each other. The king of Akkad and his army turned back and returned to Babylon

It is however the next part of that text that provides a real insight into the nature of the damage suffered in the battle by the Babylonian army:

In the fifth year (600–599 B.C.) the King of Akkad stayed in his own land and gathered his chariots and horses in great numbers.

The inference is clear; Nebuchadnezzar suffered very heavy losses in the mobile units of his army to such a degree that any further advance into Egypt was no longer possible. The *Chronicle* speaks of 'an open battle' and undoubtedly the mobile forces of cavalry and chariotry on either side played a very major part in the battle. Headlong clashes of large numbers of cavalry and chariots, each attempting to turn the other's open flank, would have resulted in the very heavy losses spoken of. In the years since the conflict at Carchemish, Necho II had rebuilt his army and was now employing many more heavily-armoured Greek mercenary troops. The clash, on the very borders of Egypt itself, would have imparted a sense of resolve that would have made the Pharaoh's army fight with a fervour that compensated for the reputation of invincibility which preceded Nebuchadnezzar's army in the field. The result was probably a draw.

However, Migdol was no Carchemish. The headlong flight of the Egyptian troops following that battle in northern Syria some six years before finds no parallel here. The ruthless and relentless pursuit by the Babylonian army was not repeated; there seems to have been no attempt by the Egyptian forces to harry the retreating Babylonians.

Abandoning the battlefield to the severely battered Egyptians – who were thus able to claim a victory, albeit Pyrrhic – the Babylonian monarch conducted an orderly withdrawal into Palestine. After leaving troops in the garrison towns of Syria, he retired with the bulk of the army to Babylon in order to rest and regroup. In the wake of the temporary abandonment by the Babylonians of southern Palestine, the Egyptians followed up and invested the city of Gaza. That they failed to move further up the coast and exploit fully the Babylonian withdrawal suggests that the effort expended in halting the Babylonian advance into Egypt had been at such a cost that they no longer possessed the will or wherewithal to challenge Nebuchadnezzar on land. Indeed, the occupation of Gaza marks the final attempt of Egypt to gain control of the land area of the eastern Mediterranean seaboard. It has to be seen as a tacit acceptance of the reality of Babylonian domination and control.

From the perspective of Jerusalem, however, matters were seen in a much more optimistic light. The Babylonian withdrawal presaged the return of Egypt to Palestine and thus the dearest hopes of Jehoiakim and the majority of the political establishment of Judah were being realised. Deeming the retreat of Nebuchadnezzar to be final, Jehoiakim withheld his tribute to Babylon and was, therefore, in breach of his treaty with his overlord. It was an act that within three short years was to bring about his death and the deportation of the high and mighty of the land to Babylon. It was the direct cause of more than seventy years in exile for his people.

The Fall of Jerusalem

The failure of the Babylonian King to react directly against Judah in the year following Jehoiakim's rebellion must have been seen as a good sign to the Jews. However, Nebuchadnezzar returned to the Hatti-land in late 599 B.C. in order to deal with caravan raiders.

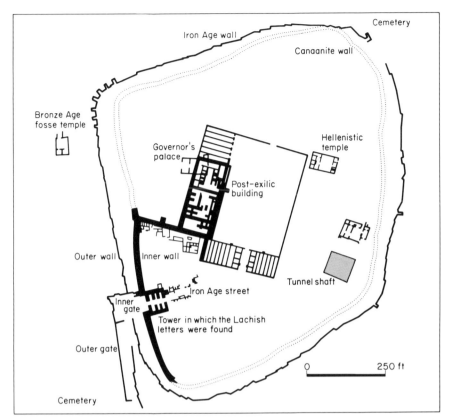

Iron Age wall
Cemetery
Canaanite wall
Bronze Age
fosse temple
Governor's
palace
Hellenistic
temple
Post-exilic
building
Outer wall
Inner wall
Iron Age street
Tunnel shaft
Inner
gate
Tower in which the Lachish
letters were found
Outer gate
Cemetery
0   250 ft

Once again it is interesting to note how similar were both the problems and the solutions faced by the Babylonians and the Assyrians before them. Less than fifty years earlier, Assurbanipal had sent units of the Assyrian army into the desert to destroy the tented settlements and plunder the waterholes of the Arabs. Nebuchadnezzar adopted an identical strategy. From the garrison bases of Carchemish, Riblah and Hamath, he despatched his own troops into the desert in an operation that would be described in the parlance of modern counter-insurgency warfare as a 'search and destroy' mission.

Seemingly at his leisure, Nebuchadnezzar invoked the terms of the treaties with his vassals and ordered them to attack and harrass the borders of Judah. In conjunction with auxiliary Babylonian forces based in southern Syria, the Aramaeans, Moabites and Ammonites began a campaign against Judah from the north and the east that must have done much to drain the military resources of the Jewish state. The continual raiding caused an influx into Jerusalem of people seeking safety. One such group were the Rechabites, the archetypal abstainers from the vine, whose descendants in 'spirit', are still with us.

In the following year, however, the Babylonian army itself moved against Judah. In all probability it was only a short time after the events of the year 597 B.C. that a scribe at the court of Nebuchadnezzar in Babylon

This reconstructed plan of Lachish, the fortified city to the south west of Jerusalem, is based upon archaeological excavation and thus shows several major periods of occupation. It is where the important Ostraca, the 'Lachish letters' were found.

121

was ordered to record the campaign. Preparing a small tablet of damp clay and taking up his *qan tuppi* or reed-stylus, he inscribed on it in cuneiform the formal account in the *Chronicle* of the operations against Al Yahudu, the city of Judah:

In the seventh year, in the month of Kislev, the Babylonian king mustered his troops, and having marched to the land of Hatti, besieged the city of Judah, and on the second day of the month of Adar took the city and captured the king. He appointed therein a king of his choice, received its heavy tribute and sent them to Babylon.

Capture of the City

The Bible has nothing to say about the seeming rapidity of the Babylonian advance on Jerusalem. Nebuchadnezzar had mustered his army in Babylon during the November of 598 B.C. and within a matter of three months had taken the city. There can be no doubt that the specific mention of Jerusalem, as 'the city of Judah', means that its reduction and capture was the main task of that year's operations in the west. Nebuchadnezzar was not a man to embark upon the task of laying siege to a city with defences as powerful as those of Jerusalem without very careful preparation. Over a century before, King Sennacherib had been frustrated in his efforts to take the city. The Assyrians, who had a justifiable reputation for ruthless efficiency when it came to siege warfare had to satisfy themselves with the destruction of the lesser fortress of Lachish. It is unlikely that in 597 B.C. the defences of Jerusalem were any less strong than when Sennacherib had laid siege. So why did it fall so rapidly?

The Babylonian army that moved against Jerusalem did so fully prepared for a long siege. No doubt Nebuchadnezzar had spent the time since Jehoiakim's revolt making careful preparations to punish his rebellious vassal. Knowledge of the city's defences would have been acquired and to this, intelligence would have been added that concerned the state of Judah's own army. Additionally, the attacks of the Ammonites, Moabites and Aramaeans over the preceding years may well have been part of a longer term strategy to 'bleed' the Judaean forces before he invaded. Little notice seems to have been taken of the possibility of Egyptian intervention.

Death of Jehoiakim

Ultimately, the explanation for the rapid fall of Jerusalem must be seen in terms of the changed political circumstances brought about by the death of Jehoiakim in December 598 B.C. However, different sources give conflicting accounts of the demise of this monarch. The *Second Book of Kings* (24:6) speaks of him dying a natural death.

On the other hand the *Second Book of Chronicles* (36:7) has a varying account of his fate: 'Nebuchadnezzar, king of Babylon attacked him, loaded him with chains and took him to Babylon'.

Nevertheless, it is accepted by most commentators that Jehoiakim died a natural death some three months before Jerusalem fell to Nebuchadnezzar and that he was succeeded by his son Jehoiakin.

It was not an enviable time for a young man to assume the mantle of kingship, and his reign was very short. On 15–16th March 597 B.C., in the company of his mother, his retinue, his nobles and his officials, he went out from the city and surrendered to Nebuchadnezzar.

We have no source that tells us why Jehoiakin felt it necessary to surrender. There is simply no way of corroborating the statement made by Flavius Josephus in his *Jewish Antiquities* to the effect that Nebuchadnezzar gained an entrance to Jerusalem by falsely promising Jehoiakin leniency, but then changed his mind and laid siege to the city.

Perhaps the Egyptians indicated that they were not prepared to help, and the arrival of Nebuchadnezzar in person finally brought the young king to the view that only by throwing himself on the mercy of the Babylonian monarch could Jerusalem be spared the horrors of a prolonged siege. Whatever the reason the *Second Book of Kings* states clearly that Jehoiakin: 'surrendered to the king of Babylon, and the king of Babylon took them prisoner in the eighth year of his reign.'

The gates of the great city were thrown open and the Babylonian troops entered to begin the task of assessing the spoil and booty to be taken back to Babylon.

The Lachish Ostraca. These drawings illustrate two of the shards of pottery excavated from the site of the main gate at Lachish, the fortified city to the south west of Jerusalem. On them, inscribed in Hebrew, is correspondence between two officers in the Judaean army concerning incidents occurring during the time of the Babylonian siege of Jerusalem.

Deportation

From amongst the population of Jerusalem, swollen by the many thousands who had fled to the city for safety in the face of the Babylonian advance, the officers of the Great King selected those who would be deported to Babylon. The description of the Babylonian treatment of Jerusalem found in the Bible well illustrates the price paid by the people of Judah for their ill-fated rebellion against their Babylonian overlord:

The latter [the Babylonians] carried off all the treasures of the temple of Yahweh and the treasures of the palace and broke up all the golden furnishings which Solomon the king had made for the sanctuary of Yahweh . . . He carried all Jerusalem off into exile, all the nobles and all the notables, ten thousand of these were exiled, with all the blacksmiths and metalworkers; only the poorest people in the country were left behind. He deported Jehoiakin to Babylon, as also the king's mother, his officials and the nobility of the country; he made them all leave Jerusalem for exile in Babylon. All the men of distinction, seven thousand of them, the blacksmiths and metalworkers, one thousand of them, all the men capable of bearing arms, were led off into exile in Babylon by the king of Babylon.

(2 Kings 24:13–16)

However, there is some uncertainty as to the exact number of deportees. Jeremiah gives a much smaller figure of three thousand and twenty three

Judaeans for the deportation of 597 B.C. Indeed he quotes figures for the two later deportations, in 586 and 581, that taken in addition to those he gives for the first deportation in 597 B.C. total less than one half of those spoken of in the *Book of Kings*.

Policy and Purpose

The Babylonian policy of dealing with recalcitrant vassals was, not surprisingly, very similar to that adopted by the Assyrians. The motives in either case stemmed from security considerations and economic gain.

In the case of the former, it was assumed that by deporting the leading elements of the population – the King, nobility, senior military figures and the temple priesthood – the defeated vassal was deprived of those in the country most likely to sponsor rebellion. A process of political decapitation rendered the kingdom much more amenable to the wishes of the overlord. In addition, the psychological blow of the deportations was sufficient to 'break the will' of those who were left and remove any desire to translate residual nationalist sentiment into further rebellion.

It would be wrong, however, to imagine the actual process of deportation as being like the 'death march' on Bataan in World War 2. Certainly, on the 'long trek' to Babylon, people must have died; but it seems this was a consequence more of the distance involved and the rigours of the climate than any deliberate policy of deprivation by the Babylonians. Indeed, bearing in mind that the deportees were seen by their conquerors as an economic resource, it is not surprising that considerable care was exercised in ensuring that as many prisoners as possible arrived in good condition.

The selection for deportation of artisans alongside the 'high and mighty' of the land demonstrates the way that Nebuchadnezzar intended to use the skills and expertise of Judaean blacksmiths and metalworkers. In being set to work in the great city, these craftsmen found themselves employing their expertise alongside others from Tyre, Sidon, Elam and Syria, who had like themselves been deported following the capture of their cities or who had been taken to Babylon as part of the annual tribute levied upon his vassals by Nebuchadnezzar. Their task was one of transforming Babylon into the greatest city in the world.

Great Babylon

Whilst the Kings of Assyria revelled in their imperial conquests and in the martial ardour of their armies, the Kings of Babylon, whilst no less committed to the imperial drive for conquest and expansion, left no lasting monuments as a testimony to their wars or the prowess of their arms. It is possible to wander through galleries in a number of the

world's major museums and gain a remarkable insight into the formidable instrument of aggrandisement that was the Assyrian army and gauge from the care taken over the rendering of even the smallest detail of military equipment that here was where the 'heart and treasure' of the Kings of Assyria lay. In stark contrast, it is only on the building bricks that litter Babylon that we perceive the real concerns of Nebuchadnezzar and his successors.

Designating himself the: 'Provider of Esagila and Ezida', Nebuchadnezzar tells us that his pride lay in his service to the gods and in the provision of fine cities within which they might dwell. It was in his building achievements that Nebuchadnezzar seems to have gained his greatest satisfaction. His expansionist policy cannot be seen as distinct from the task of rebuilding Babylon; it was a matter intimately related to his ability to achieve that policy. Indeed, even a century and more after his death Herodotus could say of his labour that Babylon 'surpasses in splendour any city of the known world'. The imperial policy and his frequent campaigns in the west were unambiguously directed by Nebuchadnezzar towards acquisition of booty and manpower that could be used in the building work in Babylon. The rationale for the deportation policy shows how carefully Babylonian officers set about rounding up artisans with specific skills. This was no arbitrary policy but one conceived with distinct building needs in Babylon in mind. This underlying purpose of the Babylonian King was an essential part of his conquests, as in the 'liberation' of the 'hardy, tall, stout cedars of the Lebanon' and the evident satisfaction he expressed that they would be employed in the service of 'Marduk my king'. In this case they were

A small section from the Lachish wall relief depicting the Assyrian King Sennacherib's siege of that city in 705 B.C. It shows a group of Judaean prisoners beginning the long march into exile. The deportations carried out by the Babylonians over a century later would have looked little different.

plainly destined to be used in the refurbishment of the roofing and gates of the shrines of the major gods of Babylon. Whilst space is not available here to give a fully detailed history and description of Babylon itself, an account of the rebuilding of Babylon by Nebuchadnezzar tells us something of the man himself and so requires some insight, however small, into the object of his labours.

The City

At the time of Nebuchadnezzar the city of Babylon was bisected by the River Euphrates. On the eastern bank lay what was called the 'old city'. The walls which enclosed this area were rather more than a mile long and formed an irregular square within which were the most important buildings. It is this part of the city that has received the greatest attention from the archaeologists. Whilst it is known that Nebuchadnezzar extended the walls westwards to embrace the settlement on the other bank, little is actually known in detail concerning this part of the city as much of it is now underneath the present bed of the Euphrates, the course of which has moved westward since Neo-Babylonian times.

Defensive Walls

Two sets of fortifications enclosed the city. The inner fortifications are those referred to already as enclosing the 'old city' and the settlement on the western bank. The outer city wall was begun by Nabopolassar and completed by his son, but only covered the eastern bank. Together they formed a formidable defensive system of considerable complexity.

The Inner Wall was in reality two walls, one within the other. The 'inner wall' had a thickness of 21 feet and was higher than the 'outer' wall, whose thickness was about 12 feet. They were separated by a space of 24 feet filled with earth. On top was constructed a military roadway, at parapet level and wide enough (according to Herodotus) to allow a four-horse chariot to pass. Both of these walls had crenellated battlements and at intervals along the walls were towers. On the inner part of the wall they were spaced every 59 feet whilst on the outer part of the wall and at a lower level they were spaced every 67 feet. Outside of this Inner Wall was an encircling moat constructed on the inner face of strong kiln-baked bricks set in bitumin. The source of the water for this canal was, of course, the Euphrates itself. Built into the Inner Wall were nine gates named after the gods of the city, of which the most famous was the Ishtar Gate named for the goddess of love. Clearly these gates opened out onto bridges that crossed the canal and provision must have been made when they were built to allow them to be raised or dealt with by some other means in the event of a siege. Each gate itself was very heavily fortified and the massive programme was embarked upon: 'In order to strengthen the defences of Esagila that the evil and the wicked might not oppress Babylon.'

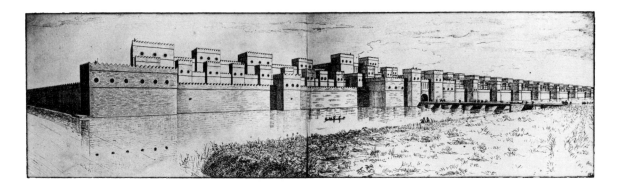

The Outer Wall was also a double wall which began a mile-and-a-half to the north of the Ishtar Gate on the east bank. It ran south-easterly to a point roughly parallel with the Temple of Esagila in the 'old city'. It then turned south-westwards to meet the Euphrates a quarter of a mile south of the defensive inner system. In total, these two great walls embraced an area of some 850 hectares and could contain up to 200,000 men.

An artist's impression of the appearance of the inner fortifications of Babylon on the western side of the city. Clearly shown are the crenellated fortifications designed to withstand prolonged siege. The picture conveys a powerful image of the strength of Babylon's defences.

Temples and Ziggurats

Nabopolassar and Nebuchadnezzar both expended much time and wealth in the refurbishment of the temples that made Babylon so important as a religious cult centre.

Of the many temples and other religious buildings in a city in which there were hundreds of shrines, two in particular are outstanding; the great ziggurat of Entemenanki and the temple complex of Esagila.

At the time Nabopolassar and his son set to work to rebuild the ziggurat it still exhibited the great damage caused to it by Sennacherib's destruction of much of the city in 689 B.C. Entemenanki, 'the building which is the Foundation of Heaven and Earth', took many years to rebuild. The completed ziggurat rose to a height of nearly 300 feet and dominated the view of the city. Its base at its maximum extent was a square with sides of about 300 feet. The main mass of the ziggurat was composed of trodden clay although the outer casing was composed of burnt brick nearly 50 feet thick. The first and second levels were reached by a staircase about 30 feet wide although the appearance of the upper storeys is uncertain and artists' reconstructions are at best tentative.

An immense labour was required to rebuild the ziggurat and many men deported to Babylon were employed on it. Nebuchadnezzar mentions that a number of kings exiled in the city, including Jehoiakin, were made to symbolically carry a corvée basket at the foundation ceremony.

The small building which topped the ziggurat and which was the 'dwelling place' of Marduk was faced by blue enamelled bricks which caused the topmost stage 'to shine like the heavens themselves'. The completion of the rebuilding of Entemenanki was a time of great festivity and rejoicing.

A plan view of Babylon under Nebuchadnezzar, in the sixth century B.C., showing the major work of construction undertaken by him and his father Nabopolassar.

Map labels: Palace of Nebuchadnezzar II, Canal, (Suburb), Canals, Canal, Euphrates, Akitu house, Main Citadel, Outer city wall, Marduk gate, Kish, Lugalgirra gate, Southern citadel, Belit Nina temple, Banitu, Gate, Adad temple, Nukhar, Shamash temple, Shamash gate, Tombs, Burial grounds, Tuba, Litamu, Urash gate, New canal town, Canal, 0 2000 4000 ft

1. Esagila
2. Entemenanki (ziggurat)
3. Temple of Gula
4. Hanging gardens
5. Holy gate
6. Ishtar gate
7. Temple of Ishtar
8. Temple of Ninmakh
9. Temple of Ninurta
10. Processional way

Palaces

At the time of Nebuchadnezzar there were three principal palaces known as the Northern, Southern and Summer palaces. Of these, it was the southern palace that was the most important. A very extensive building, it functioned not just as a royal residence but also as an administrative centre. The design was built around five courtyards, each one used by the King's secretariat, and included the King's private rooms, the state rooms, the garrison and the harem. In the north-eastern part of this palace the archaeologists came upon a structure that may well have been the famous Hanging Gardens of Babylon. In the vaulted chambers that underpinned this structure tablets listing the issue of grain and oil mention the name of Jehoiakin of Judah.

The Processional Way

The most famous of the many streets of Babylon was the Processional Way. Running along the eastern side of the Southern palace it was onto

In August–September 587 B.C., Jerusalem fell to Nebuchadnezzar's army after a two-year siege. Deportation and systematic destruction left the city a devastated and desolate ruin.

A modern reproduction of the Ishtar Gate built at Babylon by the Iraqi Department of Antiquities. Like its German counterpart, which is located at the Voderasiatisches Museum in Berlin, this is not a full-size replica. The original was wide enough to allow the passage of heavy, four-horsed chariots.

the Processional Way that the statues of Marduk and the other gods were brought out from Esagila to be borne through the magnificent Ishtar Gate to the Akitu House at the time of the New Year Festival. Approaching Babylon from the north via the Ishtar Gate one would pass along the Processional Way between high walls. Each wall was lined with the figures of lions moulded in glazed brick. On the road surface itself Nebuchadnezzar laid large limestone flags flanked by slabs of red breccia veined with white.

The Ishtar Gate itself was double, running the width of both fortification walls. The gate was decorated with glazed tiles depicting 150 bulls and Sirrush dragons. The colour of the background tiles was a very vivid blue with the bulls and dragons appearing alternately in white and yellow.

Even this very short description of Babylon communicates something of the magnificence of the city in the time of Nebuchadnezzar. Perhaps then we can understand the words attributed to the Great King himself:

Great Babylon! Was it not built by me as a royal residence by the force of my might and for the majesty of my glory

(Daniel 4:27)

Twenty-three centuries later the product of such great labour is slowly being reclaimed from the earth that 'swallowed' it up. In the ruins uncovered by the careful and diligent work of the archaeologists, it is still possible to discern the greatness of Babylon and sense the power and majesty of its greatest architect and builder.

A King of His Own Choice

Nebuchadnezzar was able to maintain his new realms whilst Babylon flourished. In the place of Jehoiakin, who was to spend the rest of his days in exile, Nebuchadnezzar chose the youngest son of Josiah, the former king. However, to demonstate that his elevation to the kingship of Judah was in the gift of the King of Babylon, Nebuchadnezzar had the successor's name changed from Mattaniah to Zedekiah, which means 'Yahweh-is-my-justice'. It was chosen to symbolize that, in taking his oath of fealty to his overlord, Zedekiah had called upon Yahweh to witness his declaration of loyalty.

The gods of Babylon had also been invoked to witness that Zedekiah had declared to Nebuchadnezzar that he would 'surely keep the country for him and attempt no uprising nor show friendliness to the Egyptians'. The final part of the vassal treaty required a recital of the ritual curses that would be invoked if Zedekiah broke the terms of the treaty.

However, the harsh punishment that would inevitably fall on the head of the Judaean King and his people was no arbitrary destruction exercised by an aggrieved monarch. Rather, the gods of Babylon and the God of

A close-up of one of the many bulls depicted on the Ishtar Gate and whose glazed finish of yellow alternating with white, on a vivid blue background, caused the whole edifice to blaze in the sunlight. The other creature to appear on the Gate was the mythological Sirrush dragon. A hybrid creature with the head and horns of the Arabian viper, front legs of a cat and the rear of a bird of prey, the tip of its tail has a scorpion's sting.

Judah, seeing the treaty broken by the very supplicant who had called upon them to witness his profession of loyalty, would demand vengeance upon him and would call upon the King of Babylon to be at once their arbiter and also the instrument of their punishment. It was because Zedekiah was Nebuchadnezzar's man on the throne of Judah that any future rebellion would be suppressed with harshness so severe that the continued existence of the throne of David was in danger.

Zedekiah's Weakness

It was a tragedy for Judah that Nebuchadnezzar's 'king of his own choosing' was so ill equipped for the task. Jehoiakim had been a headstrong, arrogant ruler but Zedekiah was from a different mould. A weak, mild-mannered and vacillating man, his self-confidence was undermined almost from the beginning by his realization that many in Judah still regarded Jehoiachin as the legitimate ruler of the land. In the end it was his own character defects and weaknesses that led directly to the débâcle of 587 B.C. with many in opposition to the will of Nebuchadnezzar.

As was his custom Nebuchadnezzar returned quickly to Babylon following the conclusion of the Judaean campaign. He had left behind him a people dazed and bewildered by the events of the previous few months. From within the context of their religious ideology, the unthinkable had happened: Jerusalem the inviolable had indeed been violated. How was this to be explained when Yahweh's temple, the sanctuary of the Lord, itself gave protection to Jerusalem?

Seeds of Defiance

In 593 B.C. the accession of Psammetichus II to the throne of Egypt led to a revival amongst the pro-Egyptian leadership in Judah who hoped that the new Pharaoh intended to challenge Babylonian control in Palestine. In anticipation, the rulers of Edom, Ammon, Moab, Tyre and Sidon sent their representatives to a conclave in Jerusalem to discuss the formation of an anti-Babylonian alliance. It was then that Jeremiah, in accord with the wishes of his God, picketed the meeting and having donned thongs and yokes, the symbols of submission, called on the assembled representatives to forgo their plans for rebellion.

In one of the personal and secret meetings that the prophet had with the King, he repeated the same message: rebellion was doomed to failure; it was Yahweh who had ordered that events be so; how could he therefore even contemplate rebellion knowing what he did?

Zedekiah displayed great indecision in response. Then, two events occurred that led the anti-Babylon faction to press ahead with plans to rebel. Pharaoh Psammetichus led a successful campaign into Nubia and in 591 B.C. made an expedition to Palestine, ostensibly for religious reasons. Following so soon after his triumph of arms in the south, the

event must have been interpreted as more than just a symbolic re-assertion of traditional Egyptian claims in the area. The failure of Nebuchadnezzar to make any appearance in Syria–Palestine since 594 B.C. must also have led some to interpret this as a sign of growing Babylonian weakness. To many in Judah the time seemed right to throw off the yoke of Babylon.

The End of Judah

The Bible itself has nothing to say concerning the reasons for Zedekiah's rebellion against Nebuchadnezzar. Nevertheless, one must conclude that he had been given cause to believe that Egyptian help would be forthcoming to counter the inevitable Babylonian response. It is only in this light that any sense can be made of his decision to declare formally his state of rebellion by withholding payment of tribute. The prophet Ezekiel alluded to this by making reference to the faithlessness of Zedekiah, who in breaking his oath to Nebuchadnezzar forgot that he had invoked the name of Yahweh, his God, to witness his profession of loyalty to the Babylonian monarch.

The date of the rebellion cannot be fixed with any certainty although it seems likely that Zedekiah was in violation of his oath of submission to his overlord by at least 589 B.C. Whatever, the response of

This small section of the Babylonian Chronicle records in cuneiform, the account of Nebuchadnezzar's taking of the city of Jerusalem in 597 B.C. Mentioned is the deportation of Jehoiakin and the installation of Zedekiah, 'the King of his own choice', as the new ruler of Judah.

Nebuchadnezzar was swift and harsh. In 588, the Babylonian army entered Judah bringing fire and destruction to the land, intent on just retribution for the rebellion of the vassal state. The doom of the kingdom and the end of the throne of David, which had so long been prophesied by Jeremiah, were at last at hand.

Under Siege

The Babylonian army moved rapidly to invest Jerusalem itself. In a manner reminiscent of the Assyrian campaign against Judah in 701 B.C., the Babylonians surrounded the city with a ring of extensive earthworks to enclose the population in order to prevent their coming or their going. Plainly, their intended strategy was to starve the city into surrender.

From the wall of the city, Zedekiah would have looked down upon the enemy soldiers struggling hard in the hot sun to throw up the earthworks. Already the familiar view beyond the city would be changing as the hordes of Babylonian troops cut down every available tree to underpin the great earth ramps that formed part of the surrounding ring. The horrors of siege warfare were a contemporary fact of life, but to the King and others contemplating the labour of the Babylonians, the first doubts as to the wisdom of their actions must have begun to enter their minds. In the great Temple of Solomon the daily sacrifices and rituals continued, but now there was an added sense of urgency in the supplications of the priests in their prayers to Yahweh. But Zedekiah already knew from the mouth of Jeremiah that Yahweh was deaf to the prayers of the people, oblivious to the sacrifices made in his name.

With the city fully invested, a token force of soldiers was left to guard the perimeter while the bulk of the army moved out into the highlands of Judah to begin a campaign designed to devastate the entire country. One by one, the towns of the land were subjected to fire and destruction. From Gibeah in the north to Arad in the south, and from Eglon in the west to En-Gedi in the east, the Babylonian army systematically set about destroying the major settlements of Judah. The archaeological record well attests to the savagery of the Babylonian onslaught.

From his base at Riblah, Nebuchadnezzar received regular reports from his senior commanders in the field concerning the progress of the campaign. Unlike the short siege of 597 B.C., he was not present at all during the second siege. The position of Riblah, with its good communications to the south, allowed him to be informed rapidly of events in Judah whilst overseeing the continued operations in the thirteen-year-long siege of Tyre. It was here that he received news of the advance along the coast of an Egyptian army towards Gaza.

It seems that only after Zedekiah made a direct appeal to Apries, the new Pharaoh of Egypt, was help from this quarter forthcoming. Among a number of messages scribbled on potsherds (discovered near the gate of the fortress of Lachish during the excavations of the Wellcome–Marston expedition in the 1930s) there is one that refers to the despatch to Egypt of a General Konyahu, son of Elnatan. It is possible that Konyahu was the head of the military delegation sent by Zedekiah to Apries to request Egyptian military help. The force despatched by the Pharaoh gave, at best, a temporary respite to those besieged in Jerusalem. The Babylonian forces surrounding the city temporarily abandoned the siege lines and deployed for battle against the Egyptian forces in the area of Gaza. Whether or not the two opposing armies met in battle is uncertain. What is clear, however, is that the Egyptian army withdrew again into Egypt after tentative probings. Thereafter, no Egyptian aid was forthcoming. Patently, Pharaoh Apries had abandoned Judah to its fate.

Prophesy of Doom

The withdrawal of the Babylonian army to deal with the Egyptian incursion seemed to many in Jerusalem to be a hopeful sign. Zedekiah sent a delegation to the prophet Jeremiah with the request that he intercede with Yahweh to save the city. But Jeremiah had no words of balm or hope for the King, only the same message of unrelenting doom.

The respite gained by the Babylonian withdrawal provided the opportunity to ease the desperate food situation. This could have been no easy task as the Babylonian army itself was living off the land. Even in those areas that had been spared from the 'scorched earth' campaign of the

The ruins of Nebuchadnezzar's great palace in Babylon, known to the German archaeological team who excavated it as the 'Southern Citadel'.

Babylonian soldiery, the available supplies would have gone first to serve the needs of the army. Those Judaeans in the countryside who had survived the initial Babylonian onslaught must have been living in the most desperate of circumstances.

It was also during this interregnum that Jeremiah, while preparing to leave the city, was arrested on the grounds that he was deserting to the enemy. There were many amongst the King's retinue who wanted Jeremiah executed as his continual pronouncements of Jerusalem's fall were undermining morale amongst the soldiers and the people. The weak and vacillating monarch, a puppet of his advisers, handed the prophet over with a comment that provides an insight into the true state of affairs within the Judaean court: 'He is in your hands as you know, for the King is powerless to oppose you'. So taking Jeremiah they lowered him into the cistern of the King's son Malchiah and left him to die. He was rescued by an Ethiopian servant of Zedekiah who had appealed to the King to allow him to save the prophet. Jeremiah was then taken to the Court of the Guard for safe keeping. It was while he was here that Zedekiah summoned Jeremiah for a secret meeting in the Temple.

In what was undoubtedly their last face-to-face meeting, Jeremiah tried to convince the King that even now, by throwing himself on the mercy of Nebuchadnezzar, his life and the city could be saved. However the King could only see things in terms of his own fear, afraid of his fate at the hands of those of his countrymen who had gone over to the Babylonian monarch if he surrendered. In the pathos of the moment Jeremiah told the King: 'You will not be handed over to them'.

Pleading with Zedekiah, Jeremiah then proceeded to tell him;

Please listen to Yahweh's voice as I have relayed it to you, and then all will go well with you and your life will be safe. But if you refuse to surrender, this is what Yahweh has shown me: the sight of all the women left in the king of Judah's palace being led off to the king of Babylon's generals . . . Yes, all your wives and children will be lead off to the Chaldeans, and you yourself will not escape their clutches but will be a prisoner in the clutches of the king of Babylon. As for this city, it will be burnt down.

(Jeremiah 38:20–23)

Zedekiah could not bring himself to do what the prophet asked and commanding Jeremiah to remain silent returned to his palace. But by that time the Babylonian army had returned and were taking the steps to bring the siege of Jerusalem to its bloody and desperate conclusion.

The Final Act

With the return of the Babylonian army, only Jerusalem and the fortified cities of Azekah and Lachish remained.

Azekah and Lachish both fell shortly after the Babylonian army resumed its siege of the capital. However, in the case of Lachish it is obvious from the archaeological record that its taking was no easy matter. The ferocity of the attack was such that fires set up against the city walls were so intense that the effect was startling:

masonry, consolidated into a chalky white mass streaked with red, had flowed in a liquid stream over the burnt road surface and lower wall, below which were piled charred heaps of burnt timber. In the angle below the north wall of the Bastion and the west revetment, breaches had been hurriedly repaired and any material available were forced again; indeed, evidence of destruction by fire was not difficult to find anywhere within the walls of the city.

(O. Tufnell)

The stage was now set for the final act itself – the capture of Jerusalem.

A much closer siege wall was set up by the Babylonians allowing the large siege towers that had been erected to be moved closer to the walls of Jerusalem. From these great towers, archers poured a withering fire of arrows down on to the heads of the defenders on the city walls. Below, rams proceeded to batter away at the stonework. The attack itself was concentrated on the northern wall. Certainly, the western wall of the city seems to have been too well constructed to allow the Babylonians to effect a breach.

In the fourth month of the eleventh year of Zedekiah, June–July of 587 B.C., the Babylonians breached the wall and broke into the city. For the defenders and others crowding within its walls, conditions were by now desperate. Hunger was by now gripping the city with the non-combatant population suffering the worst of the privation and what little food there was going to the soldiers. The *Book of Lamentations* paints vivid pictures of the horror of the siege for the people of Jerusalem:

> The tongue of the baby at the breast,
> stick to its palate for thirst;
> little children ask for bread,
> no one gives them any.
> Those who used to eat only the best,
> now lie dying in the streets;
> those who were reared in the purple
> claw at the rubbish heaps,
> With their own hands, kindly women
> cooked their own children,
> this was their food,
> Happier those killed by the sword,
> than those killed by famine

The Babylonians penetrated the outer wall built by King Hezekiah over a century before. Once inside Jerusalem it was only a matter of time before the 'inner city', containing the palace and great temple within the walls built during the early period of the monarchy, succumbed.

With the Babylonians inside the city walls Zedekiah made the decision to flee the city. Infiltrating the Babylonian siege lines, the Judaean forces passed into the valley of the River Jordan known as the Arabeh and headed towards Ammon, the only other state that had stood by Zedekiah in his rebellion against Nebuchadnezzar.

> The king then made his escape under cover of dark, with all the fighting men, by way of the gate between the two walls, which is near the king's garden – the Chaldeans had surrounded the city and made his way towards the Arabeh

It was a forlorn hope. The Babylonians, learning of the escape, pursued the fleeing Judaeans and captured Zedekiah in the plains of Jericho. By this time he was alone, except for possibly a few of his retinue, his troops having deserted and run for their lives. A sad, pathetic and lonely figure he was placed in chains and taken to Riblah, there to face Nebuchadnezzar in the certain knowledge that this time there would be no mercy.

Judgement of the King

At Riblah, as Jeremiah had foretold, Zedekiah was brought to Nebuchadnezzar and was condemned by the very terms of the vassal treaty he had acceded to in 597 B.C. and had invoked Yahweh to witness. A shattered man, he had to stand in the presence of the Babylonian King and watch as one by one his sons were brought in and slaughtered before his eyes.

These tragic images were the last to be inscribed on Zedekiah's memory. Almost immediately after, and in accord with the judgement of Nebuchadnezzar, burning irons put out his eyes. Dragged from the chamber, blinded and stumbling, he was loaded onto a cart and taken to Babylon, there to disappear from sight and from the pages of history into one of the dungeons of the Babylonian King.

The Sack of Zion

Following the surrender of the city, which must have occurred shortly after Zedekiah's capture, Nebuchadnezzar sent Nebuzaradan, the commander of his guard, from Riblah to oversee the systematic sacking and destruction of Jerusalem.

The Temple of Solomon was burned down and all the items of value, of gold, silver and bronze, within it were taken off to Babylon as booty. The royal palace which was part of the same complex of buildings as the temple suffered the same fate. The Babylonian objective was to ensure that no buildings suitable as strong defensive points were left standing. From the temple mount, the soldiery moved down into the city itself demolishing and burning all the 'great houses' belonging to the nobility, destroying any building that could serve as a potential point of resistance. Finally, the walls themselves were pulled down. Over a century later, in 446 B.C. Nehemiah, returning to the city was able to say 'Jerusalem is in ruins and its gates burnt down'.

Babylonian destruction of the city and of all the major towns and cities of the land had been such that for those survivors not deported, existence was in all probability reduced to a subsistence level. These poor people were left behind to tend the vineyards and to plough the land – but the kingdom of Judah, which had survived for some four hundred years from the time of David, was ended.

Just inside the city walls of Babylon, by the Ishtar Gate, are these ruins of the temple dedicated to the god Ninmakh.

Legacy of Exile

Nebuchadnezzar died in 562 B.C. after a reign of forty-two years. His son and successor Amel-Marduk released Jehoiakin from his imprisonment and had him eat from the royal table.

The majority of Jewish captives were settled in communities alongside the Chebar River. Unlike the Assyrians, who did everything possible to break down the national identity of their deported populations, the Babylonians allowed the Jews and others to retain their distinctive religious and national identities. Many found the experience of exile from the pleasant land very difficult to come to terms with:

> *By the rivers of Babylon*
> *we sat and wept*
> *at the memory of Zion.*
> *On the poplars there*
> *we had hung our harps*
> *For there our gaolers had asked us*
> *to sing them a song,*
> *our captors to make merry,*
> *'Sing us a song of Zion'*
> *How could we sing a song of Yahweh*
> *on alien soil?*
>
> (Psalms 137:1–4)

It was here, in the absence of the Temple, that the first meeting places or synagogues were established in order that the scriptures could be read. It was a great period of activity for the Jewish people; old traditions were rethought and rewritten. Out of the experience of the exile, a new insight into the faith of their fathers was born.

When the Jewish exiles were at last allowed to return home, by permission of the Persians, the new masters of Babylon, they carried with them ideas and thoughts that would change the world.

For many, the enduring symbol of Babylon is the basalt lion, first uncovered by Arab villagers in 1776. Shown mauling a victim, the sculpture was apparently unfinished.

Chronology of Events

627 B.C.   Death of Assurbanipal, King of Assyria. Accession to throne of Ashur-etil-ilani.

626 B.C.   Nabopolassar seizes power in Babylon; in November is crowned King of Akkad. Civil war in Assyrian Empire when Sin-shar-ishkun (other son of Assurbanipal) challenges his brother for the throne of Assyria.

625 B.C.   Cyaxares, King of Media defeats the Scythians, rulers of the Medes since around 652 B.C. Nabopolassar begins diplomatic overtures to Medes for joint military action against Assyria.

623 B.C.   Sin-shar-ishkun secures Assyrian throne. Remains King until his death in 612 B.C..

620 B.C.   First mention of Nebuchadnezzar as eldest son of Nabopolassar in connection with rebuilding ziggurat of Entemenanki in Babylon.

616 B.C.   Nabopolassar begins operations against Assyrians, who are supported by Egyptian forces.

614 B.C.   Medes and Babylonians sack Assur. Alliance between Cyaxares of Media and Nabopolassar concluded. Sealed by marriage of Nebuchadnezzar to Amytis, daughter of Median king.

612 B.C.   Fall of Nineveh. Rump of Assyrian army retreats to Harran. Ashur-ubalit crowned last King of Assyria.

610 B.C.   Medes and Babylonians sack Harran. Nebuchadnezzar assumes first military command.

609 B.C.   Pharaoh Necho II gives full-scale support to remnants of Assyrian forces. Taking his army into Syria defeats army of Judah and kills King Josiah at Megiddo. Deprives Jehoahaz of Judah's throne and makes Jehoiakim King in his place.

607 B.C.   Nebuchadnezzar undertakes first independent campaign as army commander.

605 B.C.   As Crown Prince, Nebuchadnezzar assumes full command of Babylonian army in Syria. Decisively defeats Necho II at Battle of Carchemish.

604 B.C.   Nebuchadnezzar marches into Palestine. Takes city of Ashkelon after siege and receives submission of Jehoiakim, who becomes vassal of Babylon.

600 B.C.   Jehoiakim rebels against Nebuchadnezzar by failing to render tribute.

598 B.C.   Jehoiakim dies; succeeded by his son Jehoiakin.

597 B.C.   Nebuchadnezzar invades Judah. Jehoiakin surrenders and with many other Judaeans is deported to Babylon. Nebuchadnezzar chooses Mattaniah, uncle of Jehoiakin, as Judah's new King. Changes his name to Zedekiah.

590 B.C.   Zedekiah rebels against Nebuchadnezzar.

588 B.C.   Nebuchadnezzar invades Judah and lays siege to Jerusalem.

587 B.C.   Jerusalem falls to Babylonian army. Zedekiah blinded and sent to Babylon, where he dies in captivity. Jerusalem sacked and population deported.

585 B.C.   Babylonian mediation ends Lydian–Median territorial dispute in Anatolia.

581 B.C.   Third Babylonian deportation of persons from Judah.

573 B.C.   Tyre surrenders to Babylon after thirteen-year siege.

567 B.C.   Possible Babylonian invasion of Egypt.

562 B.C.   Death of Nebuchadnezzar in the forty-second year of his reign.

Bibliography

Ackroyd, P.R. *Israel under Babylon and Persia* Oxford University Press, 1986

Anderson, B.W. *The Living World of the Old Testament* Longman, 1966

Beek, M.A. *Atlas of Mesopotamia* Nelson, 1962

Bright, J.A. *History of Israel* SCM, 1981

Edwards, I.E.S. (ed) *Cambridge Ancient History* Vol III, 2 & 3, Cambridge University Press, 1975

Finegan, J. *Archaeological History of the Ancient Middle East,* Dorset, 1986

Grant, M. *The Ancient Mediterranean* Weidenfeld & Nicolson, 1969

Grant, M. *The History of Ancient Israel* Weidenfeld & Nicolson, 1984

Herodotus *The Histories* Penguin, 1986

Kenyon, K. (Revised Moorey, P.R.S.), *The Bible and Recent Archaeology* British Museum Publications, 1987

Lloyd, S. *The Archaeology of Mesopotamia,* Thames and Hudson, 1984

Miller, J.M. and Hayes, J.H. *A History of Ancient Israel and Judah* SCM, 1986

Oates, J. *Babylon* Thames and Hudson, 1986

Pritchard, J.B. (Ed) *The Ancient Near East,* Vols 1 & 2, Princeton, 1958 & 1975

Roux, G. *Ancient Iraq* Pelican, 1964

Saggs, H.W.F. *The Greatness that was Babylon* Sidgwick & Jackson, 1962

Saggs, H.W.F. *The Might that was Assyria* Sidgwick & Jackson, 1984

Walker, C.B.F. *Cuneiform* British Museum Publications, 1987

Winton-Thomas, D. (Ed) *Documents from Old Testament Times* Nelson, 1958

Wiseman, D.J. *Nebuchadnezzar and Babylon* Oxford University Press, 1983

Judas Maccabeus

REBEL OF ISRAEL

THE BATTLES OF JUDAS MACCABEUS

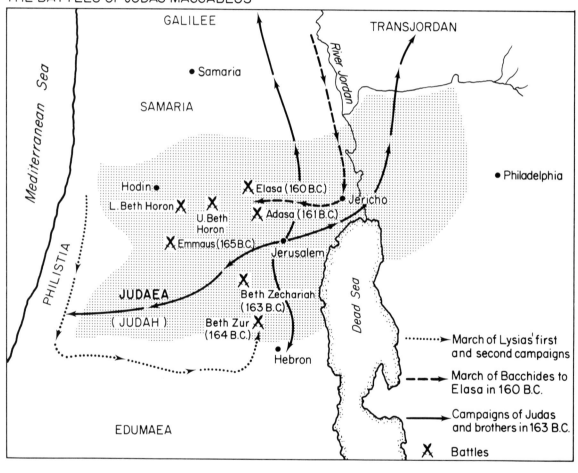

GALILEE

TRANSJORDAN

Mediterranean Sea

River Jordan

• Samaria

SAMARIA

• Philadelphia

Hodin•

L. Beth Horon ✗

U. Beth Horon ✗

✗ Elasa (160 B.C.)

✗ Adasa (161 B.C.)

• Jericho

PHILISTIA

✗ Emmaus (165 B.C.)

• Jerusalem

JUDAEA

(JUDAH)

✗ Beth Zechariah
(163 B.C.)

Beth Zur
(164 B.C.) ✗

Dead Sea

• Hebron

EDUMAEA

·······▶ March of Lysias' first
and second campaigns

━ ━ ▶ March of Bacchides to
Elasa in 160 B.C.

────▶ Campaigns of Judas
and brothers in 163 B.C.

✗ Battles

144

The man who kept Israel safe . . . the battles he fought, the exploits he performed, and all his titles to greatness have not [all] been recorded; but they were very many.

(1 Maccabees 9:19–22)

Saviour of his People

Few peoples in the world have a history as long as that of the Jews and fewer still can match the centuries of indignity, prejudice, violence and genocide directed against them. Whilst the memory of the Holocaust will never fade, the years have dimmed the knowledge that over two thousand years earlier, a similar policy of persecution was adopted that seemed aimed at nothing less than the anhiliation of the Jewish faith. It was against this backdrop of repression and genocide in the second century B.C. that Judas, the third son of Mattathias and named 'the Hammerer' emerged to save his people.

As is the case for many of the biblical heroes, he is known for his deeds rather than for what we know about him as a person. The notion of biography, of a concern for the personal details of an individual's life deemed so essential by us twentieth century moderns, was a concept alien to the Biblical writers. If such details were included it was frequently almost by 'the slip of the pen' and not deliberately.

In the case of Judas Maccabeus, we have scarcely the skeleton of biography on which to hang the flesh of his career. For a start, we do not even know how old he was when, on the death of his father in 166 B.C., he assumed the leadership of the nascent Jewish rebellion against the forces of the Seleucid empire. Yet though we know nothing definite of his appearance or of any other matters of a personal nature, we can say that he was a remarkable and charismatic figure. Apparently without any professional military experience, he ran roughshod over one of the finest military machines of the ancient world, humbling it by repeated 'hammer blows' that sent it reeling and forever dented its prestige. His battles, particularly those of his early days as a guerrilla fighter, have provided inspiration for many in a similar predicament down the ages. Indeed, when the British soldier Orde Wingate, later the founder of the Chindits, was defending Zionist settlers in Palestine in the 1930s, he used the accounts of Judas' battles in the *First* and *Second Books of Maccabees* to help plan his 'penetration' method of light infantry operations.

It is therefore in his deeds that we must look for Judas Maccabeus. The *First Book of Maccabees* is in no doubt as to the stature of the man:

He extended the fame of his people.
Like a giant, he put on the breastplate
and buckled on his war harness;
he engaged in battle after battle,
protecting the ranks with his sword.
He was like a young lion roaring over its prey
He pursued and tracked down the renegades,
he consigned those who troubled his people to the flames.
The renegades quailed with the terror he inspired
all evil doers were utterly confounded,
and deliverance went forward under his leadership.
He brought bitterness to many a king
and rejoicing to Jacob by his deeds,
His memory is blessed for ever and ever.

(1 Maccabees 3:3–7)

Crucial to an understanding of his deeds and times is some insight into the relationship between Hellenism and Judaism in the period prior to the Jewish revolt of 166 B.C. In the clash between these two seemingly incompatible cultures, and in the struggle of the Jews to assert and retain their religious and cultural identity in the face of the threat of Hellenism, lay the roots of the brutal conflict that brought forth Judas Maccabeus as the saviour of his people.

Hellenism and Judaism

When Alexander the Great died in Babylon on 10 June, 323 B.C. he bequeathed as his legacy an empire that stretched from Greece to the borders of India. The Diadochi – his successors, former generals and brothers in arms – dismembered his creation shortly after his death, and attempted to carve out their own kingdoms. Nevertheless, the cities he founded, his greatest legacy to the lands he conquered, remained. Plutarch speaks of as many as seventy, and it was in these cities that Greek culture or Hellenism was perpetuated throughout the lands of the conquest.

In Palestine, both the Ptolemies, who ruled the area between 301 and 198 B.C., and the Seleucids who succeeded them, founded many cities. These were either founded as new 'Greek' cities, with a core of Greek and Macedonian settlers, or were older settlements taken over and converted to Greek ways.

Under Antiochus III, known as 'the Great', Palestine passed under the power of the Seleucid monarchy, along with many territories in the east that were annexed in the great drive to rebuild the empire. An attempt to match this conquest in the west resulted in catastrophe at Magnesia in 190 B.C., when Antiochus was decisively defeated by the Romans.

Conflict of Cultures
The Greek language itself served as a vehicle for the transmission of Hellenistic attitudes and values. Even the Jews were not immune to the attractions of Hellenistic thought, with many forsaking the traditions of their fathers.

Yet to the traditionalists, who were critical of the new attitudes, true religion was embodied in the Torah – the first five books of the Old Testament, containing the 613 Commandments of the Law given to Moses at Sinai by God. Divine revelation had imparted to the Jewish people the true religion and the commandments to set themselves apart and have no other gods. Thus, the compromise that those in high places effected by embracing Hellenism – even though their motives had little to do with religion and much more to do with the amassing of wealth and political power – was perceived by many as a dagger aimed at the very heart of Judaism.

Thus it was a small, but powerful element in Jerusalem that attempted to make the population of Judaea adopt Hellenistic culture. That opposition to these pro-Hellenists was already evolving cannot be doubted, but it was not until the accession of Antiochus IV to the Seleucid throne in 175 B.C. and the adoption of his policies that the spark of growing antagonism was fanned into open rebellion.

Seleucus IV Philopator succeeded to the Seleucid throne on the death of Antiochus III in 187 B.C. His abortive attempt to seize the Temple treasury in Jerusalem was prompted by the need to pay the crippling war indemnity imposed by the Romans at Apamea. He was assassinated by his chief minister Heliodorus in 175 B.C.

The Mad King

Antiochus IV was the third son of Antiochus III, king of the Seleucid realm in Palestine. At an early age he had acquired a profound admiration for the institutions and policies of the Romans. This was a consequence of some fifteen years spent as their 'guest', when, following the defeat of Antiochus III at the Battle of Magnesia in 190 B.C., the young Antiochus had been sent to Rome to serve as hostage for his father. Those years had a profound effect on him. In 175 B.C., his elder brother, Seleucus IV, was required by Rome to exchange Antiochus as hostage with his second son Demetrius. Freed, the ardent young Hellenist travelled to Athens, returning with an almost evangelical commitment to the concept and spread of Hellenism. This single-mindedness, which verged on the obsessional, allied to his irrational nature, moved some to play on the name of his royal title, adopted in 169 B.C., of 'Theos Epiphanes' meaning 'God Manifest' and change it to 'Epimanes' meaning 'the Mad'.

In Athens, Antiochus cultivated a wide circle of friends and was appointed chief magistrate. Then he learned that the King's chief minister Heliodorus had brought about the assassination of his brother Seleucus IV. With the assistance of King Eumenes II of Pergamum, he therefore returned to Antioch determined to overthrow the usurper. Within a short time Heliodorus was killed and Antiochus was crowned king. All of this took place despite the fact that his nephew Demetrius was still a hostage in Rome and was the rightful heir to the throne. The consequences were to be far reaching, with Demetrius playing an important role in future events.

A passionate advocate of Hellenism, Antiochus IV sought to propogate and impose his views on his realm. His cruel and vindictive campaign against Judaism was designed to suppress all in Judaea who held beliefs he perceived as antagonistic to royal authority. This repression caused the Jewish rebellion and the emergence of Judas the Hammer.

The New Ruler

The empire that Antiochus inherited from his elder brother was in a terrible state. Many of its lands were in danger of breaking away or of being seized by other powers bent on exploiting Seleucid weakness. This weakness arose mainly from the desperate financial state of the Empire. The crippling war indemnity that Rome had imposed on Antiochus III after the Battle of Magnesia severely restricted the capacity of the Seleucid rulers to pay for armies, not only to control the lands they held but also to engage in expansion abroad. In order to fund their armies both Antiochus III and Seleucus IV had embarked on a policy of robbing temples and shrines to obtain cash. Indeed, Antiochus III met his death in the temple of Baal, near Susa in Persia, whilst levying tribute in 187 B.C. However, such a predatory policy did not always succeed. It was the abortive attempt by Seleucus IV to lay his hands on the Temple treasury in Jerusalem that contributed to the unstable situation in Judaea.

Dealing with the Realm

By 173 B.C. Antiochus had repaid the final amount outstanding to Rome and was able to deal with the internal and external problems facing his Empire. He embarked upon a deliberate policy of Hellenisation, to bring a much greater degree of coherence and order to the Empire. Simultaneously, he intended to deal with each of his enemies in turn.

He began with Egypt, for the Ptolemies of Egypt and the Seleucids had been rivals for centuries, with Palestine frequently their theatre of war. But both now had to accede to the will of Rome, the new dominant power in the Eastern Mediterranean.

By the time that Antiochus invaded Egypt for the second time in 168 B.C., he had well and truly incurred the wrath of the Roman Senate. A Roman delegation landed in Eleusis – a suburb of the city of Alexandria, outside of which Antiochus and his army were camped – to meet him and to reveal the extent of Rome's power even in the late second century B.C.

Frustration of Humiliation

The Roman ambassador, Gaius Popillius Laenas, presented himself to the King. After a few pleasantries he produced an ultimatum from the Senate, demanding that Antiochus abandon Egypt forthwith. Taken aback, the Seleucid king asked for some time to consult with his generals and advisers, all of whom were present to witness the treatment of their king. In reply, Popillius Laenas took his walking stick and, dragging it along the ground, inscribed a circle in the dust with Antiochus at its middle. He then demanded an unequivocal answer from Antiochus before he stepped from the circle.

There can be few instances in history where a military power with the symbols of its might all too visible and available has caved in totally to the threat posed by another power. There have been even fewer occasions where a monarch with pretensions to greatness – or even divinity – has been so thoroughly and completely humiliated.

The action was supremely calculated; Antiochus acceded to the Roman demand without demur. He knew what Rome could do – he had seen it for himself at Magnesia and he had no desire to court disaster. However, Seleucid dominion over Coele-Syria was confirmed so at least the King could return, assured of the integrity of the southern part of his realm, albeit 'in high dudgeon indeed and groaning in spirit, but yielding to the necessities of the time'.

The consequences of this deep humiliation were profound. Perhaps in another man the humiliation, although still deeply felt, would have been accepted; but this was Antiochus Epiphanes and many feared for the outcome.

He was a man of unpredictable moods. One moment he could be friendly and the next silent and brooding. His behaviour could be quite bizarre, and Polybius, who is a good anecdotal source, writes of him behaving in a quite Neronian manner, carousing with workmen and frequenting public baths, appearing on stage as an actor or taking part in dancing. However, the whimsy could change in a moment to a mood that was dark and threatening and which could manifest itself in cruel and fearfully vindictive behaviour almost obsessional in its desire to expend itself on an object, person or a people.

It was exactly the wrong time for a revolt in Jerusalem led by a renegade attempting to win back the office of High Priest from the Seleucid nominee. Antiochus chose to interpret the revolt as an act of rebellion and in doing so provided for himself the very means whereby he could, at a fearful cost, exorcise the frustrating humiliation inflicted upon his royal person by Gaius Popillius Laenas and the Senate of Rome.

The elephant was used extensively in war by the Seleucid forces and frequently appeared on the reverse of coins as the symbol of power. So prestigious was this symbol that it was used by Seleucid kings many years after the animals themselves were no longer employed by their armies.

Antiochus and the High Priests

When Antiochus IV had assumed the Seleucid kingship in 175 B.C., the Jews in Judaea were still living according to the decree promulgated by Antiochus III. Thereby, they were free to live according to their ancestral laws. However, the growing influence of Hellenism and the desire of many to see Judaism change to accommodate the 'new' way of thinking, led to a growing conflict over who was to be High Priest in Jerusalem.

The role of High Priest was at once both religious and political. As head of the Jewish religion, he commanded great religious prestige and was responsible for overseeing the cultus in the Temple in Jerusalem. In political terms, he was the figure to whom the Seleucid King spoke about matters of policy. It was in essence a position of great influence and power, and it was this power that was coveted by a number of priestly families strongly sympathetic to Hellenism and the Seleucids.

The High Priest in office at the time of Antiochus' accession was Onias III who held the office between 190 and 174 B.C. He was regarded by his supporters as one who remained faithful to the Law. Politically, he was hostile – albeit very diplomatically – to the Seleucids. Shortly before the death of Seleucus IV he was summoned to Antioch to account for an outbreak of violence in the city between the opposing factions and he was there when the King was assassinated.

Bribery and Corruption

Soon after seizing power in 175 B.C., Antiochus dismissed Onias and appointed a new High Priest by the name of Jason. This action by the King set a doubtful precedent; the appointment of a new High Priest had always been regarded as an internal matter for the Jews. It did not bode well for the future, for Jason had secured the position 'with a promise of three hundred and sixty talents of silver, with eighty talents to come from some other source of revenue'. Given the appetite of the Seleucid kings for money, Antiochus could hardly resist such an offer.

In order to ingratiate himself even further with the new King and to demonstrate his commitment to Hellenism, Jason then offered the King more money in return for permission to build in Jerusalem a sports centre (gymnasium) and training centre (ephebia) to impart and instil the spirit of Hellenism in the young men of the city. He further petitioned that Jerusalem and its inhabitants enjoy the same privileges as those of Antioch and be known as 'Antiochenes'. Jason was certainly not acting unilaterally in this matter. Supporting him were a group of powerful pro-Hellenists from the priestly class, as well as businessmen and merchants who hoped to benefit economically from much closer ties with the Seleucid regime.

Three years later a certain Menelaus, emulating the example set by Jason some years before, offered Antiochus 300 talents more than Jason had sent to Antioch as tribute for the King. In his turn Jason was deposed and Menelaus made High Priest. Rather than await the return of Menelaus and certain death Jason fled the city to the Trans-Jordan.

Ruthless Repression

Within a short while, however, Menelaus was in difficulty. Not only did he experience great problems in fulfilling his financial promise to the King, but of greater significance was the growing opposition to him as High Priest. Finally, insurrection broke out in the city, causing Antiochus to divert his army to Jerusalem on his return from Egypt, in order to re-assert order.

He then ordered his soldiers to cut down without mercy everyone they encountered, and to butcher all who took refuge in their houses. It was a

As head of the Jewish religion, the High Priest occupied a prestigious position of both religious and political power.

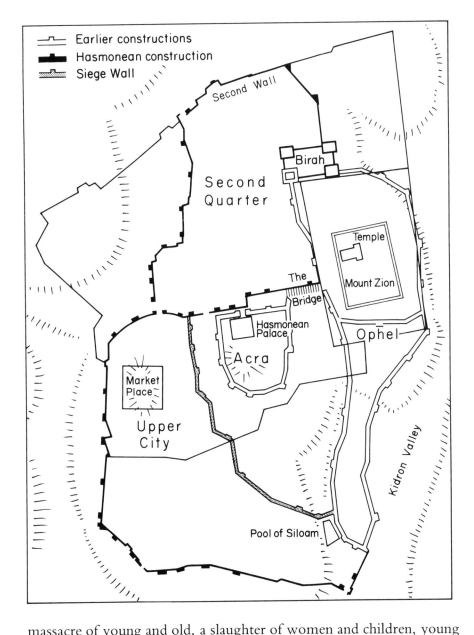

massacre of young and old, a slaughter of women and children, young girls and infants. There were eighty thousand victims in the course of three days, forty thousand dying by violence and as many again being sold into slavery.

Antiochus then pillaged the Temple, even stripping the gold plate from the façade, with the help of Menelaus and finally returned to Antioch with his booty. He left behind him in charge of the military garrison in the city a Phrygian by the name of Philip who was plainly a very ruthless individual. His brief was to prop up the rule of Menelaus with Seleucid troops.

Main features of Jerusalem during the time of the Maccabeans. Of significance is the size of the Akra (or Acra) built during the reign of Antiochus IV to house the Seleucid garrison and as a refuge for the Hellenising Jews. Judas laid seige to it unsuccessfully during the winter of 163–162 B.C.

In 168 B.C., following a rumour that Antiochus had been killed on campaign in Egypt, Jason hired a thousand mercenaries and returned to Jerusalem with the intention of reclaiming the office of High Priest. Entering the city they began their own massacre of the people in what seems to have been a senseless orgy of blood letting. The only effect was the alienation of those in the city who may have supported him against Menelaus. Driven from the city Jason went into exile and finally died in Sparta.

Once more word reached Antiochus of trouble in Jerusalem. Again he assumed it to be a rebellion, this time sending the Mysarch Apollonius with an army of 22,000 men. Apollonius waited until the Sabbath. Then, taking advantage of the Jews as they rested from work, he ordered his men to parade fully armed. All who came to watch were put to the sword. He next rushed into the city with his armed troops, and cut down an immense number of its population. On the orders of the King, the walls of the city were then dismantled and a heavily fortified base was constructed within the city. This served as a base for the garrison troops and also functioned as a kind of Greek political office, with its own institutions providing a centre within the city for the Hellenising party to continue their activities.

Judaism as the Enemy

The most sinister of the King's decrees was that which stated 'that all were to become a single people, each nation renouncing its particular customs'.

Having realised that opposition to him in Judaea was firmly rooted in the Jewish religion, Antiochus' solution to the political problem of control was to order that Judaism be proscribed. Specifically, the decree was not issued throughout the whole Seleucid Empire, but only in Judaea and directed at the Jews of that province.

With the decree began the great travail of the Jewish people. Paradoxically, this policy of enforced Hellenisation was to achieve not a quiescent people who had repudiated the faith of their fathers, but a rebellion perceived by the Jews as a battle against the forces of darkness, the consequences of which were to change the face of Judaism.

Persecution and Revolt

In the wake of the decree announcing that all 'were to become a single people', Antiochus took steps to end the ancestral worship of the Jewish people in Judaea. In all these matters he was supported by the pro-Hellenists amongst the Jews and it was with their active help that the policy against the Jewish religion in Judaea began. Yet, in the scope of the persecution were displayed a vindictiveness and cruelty which arose

A notable innovation by Antiochus IV was the conversion of some 5,000 guard infantry – the argyraspides – into heavy troops. Apart from the retention of the Thracian helmet they were armed and equipped as Roman triarii. They protected the elephants at Beth-Zechariah and equipped with pilum and scutum, had a greater degree of flexibility than the traditional Seleucid phalanx.

directly from the personality of the King. In abrogating the charter granted to the Jews by Antiochus III in 198 B.C. (in which the Law of Moses was recognised as Jewish civil law) and by re-imposing gentile practices in their place, to disobey the King's commands on these matters was made synonymous with political rebellion. Thus, to live as a gentile and disavow Jewish practices became the measure of loyalty to the Seleucid state.

Accounts are quite explicit as to the content and consequences of the King's policy:

> The king sent edicts by messenger to Jerusalem and the towns of Judah, directing them to adopt customs foreign to the country, banning burnt offerings, sacrifices and libations from the sanctuary, profaning Sabbaths and feasts, defiling the sanctuary and everything holy, building altars, shrines and temples for idols, sacrificing pigs and unclean beasts, leaving their sons uncircumcised and prostituting themselves to all kinds of impurity and abomination, so that they should forget the Law and revoke all observance of it. Anyone not obeying the king's command was to be put to death.

> (1 Maccabees 1:44–50)

As a test of their loyalty to his person and the Seleucid state, Antiochus Epiphanes had decreed that all the Jews within Judaea must sacrifice to an image like this of the Greek god Zeus, or die.

The greatest of all the abominations in the eyes of those who opposed Hellenism was the setting up on the Temple altar of an image dedicated to Olympian Zeus which bore the features of Antiochus Epiphanes himself. On this, swine's flesh was sacrificed, an act which illustrates the depth of the hatred and vindictiveness that must have inspired this persecution. Even the Greeks were not in the habit of sacrificing pigs to Zeus – this was a very special humiliation reserved, it would seem, for the Jews.

Atrocity of Repression

Many atrocities were inflicted by the Seleucid forces on the worthy people who chose death rather than forsake the Law. For example, two Jewish women were charged with having circumcised their children. They were paraded round the town, with their babies at their breasts, and then hurled over the city wall.

But perhaps no account of faith in the face of persecution is more famous than the account in the *Second Book of Maccabees* 7 which describes how a mother witnessed the martyrdom of her seven sons in a most appalling manner. Yet she comforted them with the injunction, which is one of the main theological concerns of the book, that God would not stand by and witness the persecution of his chosen people but would bring judgement on those who were the instigators of such horror and persecution.

Seeds of Revolt

Thus, it was the personality of Antiochus Epiphanes and his idiosyncratic policies that finally provided the catalyst for the Jews of Judaea to translate a growing hostility to Hellenism into armed rebellion. From the ruthless and pitiless religious persecution directed towards nothing

153

less than the total extirpation of the faith of their fathers, there emerged a war in which there could be no quarter given on either side. But it was not amongst the people of the great city that the rebellion began; it was from the hill country to the north-west of Jerusalem that the avenger of Israel was to appear.

Fire of Rebellion

The spark that ignited the flame of revolt in Judaea was the enforcement of the royal decree that all should show their loyalty to the King by swearing allegiance to his name – and to the cause he espoused. Antiochus despatched commissioners from the major centres to the outlying towns and villages. Supported by a small detachment of troops, one of these Seleucid officials journeyed from Jerusalem to Modein, a village situated in the hill country to the north-west of the city and close to the modern Israeli town of Lod. There they were to demand that the Jews, as was being required all over Judaea, make sacrifices to Dionysus and Olympian Zeus as token of their allegiance to Antiochus Epiphanes. The tactics employed by these officials were to search out the leading citizens of each area with a view to getting them to publicly acquiesce in the test of loyalty so that others, seeing their example, would follow suit. Seemingly some did indeed succumb, seduced by the bribe of being declared 'A King's Friend', a title which gave the recipient certain privileges. It was for this reason that the unnamed Seleucid commissioner sent word to the leading family of the district to present themselves at the altar already set up for the sacrifice in the middle of the town.

Calling together his five sons, Mattathias, son of Simeon and a priest of the line of Joarib, made his way to the centre of the village where a large crowd of Jews had gathered to both witness and partake in the sacrifice. Although Mattathias and his sons – John, Simon, Judas, Eleazar and Jonathan – deliberately distanced themselves from the crowd, it was to him that the Seleucid official turned first to speak:

You are a respected leader, a great man in this town; you have sons and brothers to support you. Be the first to step forward and conform to the King's decree, as all nations have done, and the leaders of Judah and the survivors in Jerusalem; you and your sons shall be reckoned among the Friends of the King, you and your sons will be honoured with gold and silver and many presents.

(1 Maccabees 2:17–18)

Plainly, the Seleucid official did not know the mettle of the man with whom he was dealing, for Mattathias' reply was unambiguous in its absolute rejection of any compromise with the decree of Antiochus:

Even if every nation living in the king's dominions obeys him, each forsaking his ancestral religion to conform to his decrees, I, my sons and my brothers will still follow the covenant of our ancestors. May heaven preserve us from forsaking the Law and its observances. As for the king's orders, we will not follow them: we shall not swerve from our own religion either to the right or to the left.

(1 Maccabees 2:19–23)

Such a reply carried a death sentence not only for Mattathias but also for his sons and kinsmen, but unlike many others of his people he was not prepared to go as a lamb to the slaughter on the blade of a gentile. Within a moment of Mattathias uttering his reply, a Jew stepped forward from the crowd with the offer that he be the first to sacrifice on the altar. This so angered Mattathias that he threw himself on the man and slaughtered him on the altar. So Antiochus Epiphanes did receive a sacrifice from Mattathias; not the one demanded but another, a human one, that of an apostate Jew!

The Cause is Born

Very quickly Mattathias and his sons fell on the surprised official and his bodyguard. Recognising the inevitable consequences of what seems to have been a completely spontaneous action, Mattathias determined that this was to be the beginning of his revolt against the Seleucid King. He proceeded to go through the town shouting out at the top of his voice: 'Let everyone who has any zeal for the Law and takes his stand on the covenant come out and follow me' (1 Maccabees 2:27).

Fleeing from Modein, Mattathias and his sons and followers escaped to the Gophna hills and esconced themselves in the area around the Beth-Horon Pass. From there they started to wage a guerrilla campaign against the Seleucid forces in the area.

It was while they were in these hills that news reached them of a massacre of their co-religionists in the desert by Seleucid forces. Apparently the group of Jews had been tracked down and surrounded in the caves in which they were sheltering. Refusing to surrender and refusing to fight on the grounds that it was the Sabbath and that fighting could be construed as work and thus forbidden by God's ordinance, they had chosen to die. The Seleucid forces broke into the caves, and the attack pressed home. Over 1000 Jews were slaughtered, with their wives, children and cattle.

As a consequence Mattathias, in his capacity as priest, ordered that fighting on the Sabbath was permitted if necessary to save 'the Law' and those who fought to protect it.

Freedom Fighters

The growing ruthlessness of the Seleucid response and the news of Mattathias' stand at Modein inspired many to flock to his cause. Of all those who did, none were more important than the Hasidim or 'pious ones'. That many of these Hasidim – 'each one a volunteer on the side of the Law' – were poor and from rural backgrounds lent an overtone of class conflict to the revolt. The rebellion very rapidly began to assume the characteristics of an all out ideological conflict, with no quarter being given by either side. With his rapidly growing body of guerrilla soldiers, Mattathias began to sweep through the hill country around Jerusalem. In

In the early days of their revolt, the Jewish guerrilla forces were simply armed. The sling was a weapon of some pedigree in their hands and wreaked fearful havoc amongst the Seleucid troops in the narrow defiles of the Judaean hills.

those areas where the Seleucid forces were unable, by virtue of the geography, to maintain more than a token presence or control, he 'cleansed' villages and towns of the trappings of the enemy. It is possible to see in the mind's eye an image of the descent from the hills, perhaps at night, and the rounding up of those deemed to be ideologically unsound. Their names procured perhaps by denunciation as collaborators, their ruthless despatch served as an example to others not to succumb to the entreaties and bribes of the enemy. Certainly the methods of ideologically motivated guerrillas, be they of a religious or political orientation, have varied little over the course of nearly two thousand years. Only the instruments with which they deal with the enemy have changed; whether one is despatched by a sword or a Kalashnikov matters little to the one who has slipped into untruth! Certainly there is nothing in the text to suggest that the ruthlessness with which Mattathias, and later Judas, eliminated those 'hostile' to the Law was thought to be wrong. On the contrary, it is condoned as the necessary means whereby zeal for the Law is made manifest in response to the dire circumstances facing the Jews. The methods were thus appropriate to the nature of the problem, for to Mattathias and his followers there could be no compromise with this enemy:

Mattathias and his friends made a tour, overthrowing the altars and forcibly circumcising all the boys they found uncircumcised in the territories of Israel. They hunted down the upstarts and managed their campaign to good effect. They wrested the Law out of the control of the gentiles and the kings and reduced the sinners to impotence.

(1 *Maccabees* 2:45–48)

Judas the Hammerer

Already old in years at the time of his revolt against Antiochus Epiphanes and realising that the exertions of campaigning had taken their toll, Mattathias knew that his death was approaching. He summoned his sons to give them his final instructions and restated what was, in essence, one of the theological themes of the *First Book of Maccabees*:

This is the time, my children, for you to have a burning zeal for the Law and to give your lives for the covenant of our ancestors.

He then asked his sons to look to their brother Simon for wise council, but in more immediate matters to follow their third brother Judas, who had already demonstrated such a remarkable prowess in war. It was to him they must look in their fight with the forces of Antiochus Epiphanes, for in him Mattathias had seen the abilities of one who could realise with a vengeance his dying words that they 'Pay back the Gentiles to the full, and hold fast to the ordinances of the Law'.

Thus it was that from the death of his father in 166 B.C. to his own demise on the battlefield of Elasa some six years later, Judas, nicknamed Maccabeus meaning the 'Hammerer', played out his short but remarkable career as the defender of the faith of his people. In that brief period of time he was to humble the armies of one of the most powerful states of the day on a number of occasions, using methods that became the inspiration of many a guerrilla fighter to this day.

Guerrilla Warrior

It is apparent from the half-hearted response of the Seleucid forces to the activities of Mattathias that they did not perceive, at first, the rebellious Jewish forces to be a real threat to their control of Judaea. This arose partly from the understandable view of the professional Seleucid soldiery, battle hardened as they were by their wars against the armies of the Ptolemies, Romans and Parthians, that an ill-equipped and, to their mind, poorly led band of religious fanatics could hardly pose a serious military threat to their power on the field of battle. In fact, the Seleucids really had little if any experience of the type of warfare that Judas, son of Mattathias now brought to bear. Guerrilla warfare is of its very nature unconventional and is dependent for its success on factors with which the professional soldiery of the day were not trained to cope.

The genius of Judas lay in his almost intuitive selection of the field of battle. He almost invariably was able to choose a site that by its very nature would negate whatever advantages the enemy had and accentuate the few material and moral qualities his own forces possessed. When on ground and at a time of his own choosing Judas Maccabeus showed – as did many others who emulated his example after him – that a guerrilla force led and inspired by a great cause could defeat a much better trained and equipped conventional army.

Strategy of Struggle
We can best understand how Judas deployed his forces or organised his guerrilla army by looking at modern guerrilla warfare, which would seem in essence to be little different to that waged by Judas. We can infer a number of things without which it certainly would not have been possible for him to fight at all.

Firstly, he must have had an extensive supply of intelligence with respect to the Seleucid forces. This was helped by the fact that they were concentrated as garrison forces in the larger towns and could easily be kept under surveillance. As is usually the case in guerrilla warfare there were many amongst the population who, whilst not willing to fight themselves, were only too happy to pass on information to Judas' camp in the mountains. This would imply that Judas was fighting for an objective that had the support of the majority of the Jewish people in Judaea. When, over twenty centuries later, Mao-Tse-Tung was to formulate the basis of successful guerrilla warfare, in stating that guerrilla

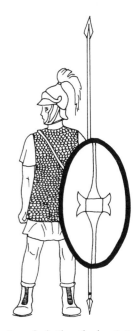

In early battles, the heaviest Seleucid troops encountered by the guerrilla fighters were probably curassiers or 'Thorakites' used to support the light infantry in the hill country. From their stripped bodies, Maccabean soldiers acquired as booty much of their weaponry and mail armour.

157

warfare was bound to fail without any political goal or if its political objectives did not coincide with the hopes of the people so that their sympathy, cooperation and assistance could not be gained.

At this very early stage of his leadership of the rebellion Judas would not have seen his cause in stark political terms, but more as a fight for religious freedom. Nevertheless, rapidly he came to realise that such religious freedom could not be sustained without the Jews securing their political independence, free from the domination of any foreign power.

It is clear that, despite the general support of the population, food and provisions were frequently in short supply in the rebel camp and hunger and exhaustion were their constant companions. Prior to the attack on the forces of Seron his men complained to Judas: 'How can we, few as we are, engage such numbers? We are exhausted as it is, not having had anything to eat today'.

We must also assume that in the early days of the rebellion the Jewish forces were poorly equipped, with the main weaponry being slings, bows and arrows, some spears and swords, and an endless supply of heavy rocks as hand projectiles. However, even this 'poor' arsenal in the hands of men with both the skill to employ such weaponry and the will to succeed can effect tremendous casualties when employed in the right conditions. In the early days that was where the guerrilla warfare of Judas Maccabeus paid dividends. Later, when attempting to take on the Seleucid forces on ground more suited to the type of warfare that was their métier, the lack of real training of the Maccabean forces led to their defeat in the full-scale, pitched battles. Nevertheless, the nature of the Seleucid forces – with their baggage trains and conventional marching order – required them to make transit through Judaea using the main ways. These frequently took them through the valleys and narrow defiles which were the perfect places for Judas to launch his attacks. It was in such circumstances that he was to realise his first victories.

The Sword of Apollonius

It was shortly after Judas assumed the leadership of the rebel forces that the first Seleucid moves were directed against him. A force was raised by Apollonius, the governor of Samaria, who, the year previously, had been despatched by Antiochus to collect tribute from the towns of Judaea. As on that occasion, he was again supported by mercenaries from Mysia – auxiliary light infantry with a scattering of light cavalry troopers.

Moving out from Samaria, the Seleucid force struck south into the forbidding hills which ran across the route to Jerusalem. Somewhere along their path Judas launched his attack.

Forewarned, probably from the moment of their departure, Judas had ample time to pick the place for his ambush. Although we have no real details about this battle, we can assume it took place in a defile and in a

Senior Seleucid officers of the army of Antiochus IV wore rich apparel and provide the likely appearance of Apollonius when he met his death at the hands of Judas Maccabeus in 166 A.D.

158

terrain where the Seleucid forces would have found it almost impossible to defend themselves against a fusillade of sling stones as they scrambled for what little cover could be found. Under a deluge of rocks, arrows and stones, the numbers of the Seleucid troops would probably have been depleted considerably before Judas gave the order to descend into the defile itself to finish them off.

With the ancient Jewish battle cry of 'Sword of the Lord' on their lips, the Maccabean fighters came down from the heights and rapidly despatched the remaining Seleucid soldiery. The few survivors – probably those at the rear of the line – managed to escape and returned with news of the disaster that had overtaken Apollonius and his men. For Judas the victory was of double benefit; spoils were seized from the dead Seleucid soldiers and Judas himself took the sword of Apollonius, a weapon he used throughout his life. For a guerrilla army, the abandoned weapons of the enemy are always the single most important source for the re-equipment of their own limited arsenal – and no doubt the sword Judas 'liberated' from Apollonius was a finely wrought and personalised weapon as befitting a man of his importance. Such acquisitions were vital, for within a short while another expedition, albeit again somewhat limited, was mounted by the Seleucids to wipe out Judas and his men.

It is clear from reports of these early Seleucid responses that the bulk of the troops stationed in the provinces of Samaria and Judaea were mercenaries of indifferent quality. This meant that Judas was not faced with the superior soldiery that comprised the main Seleucid army. The morale of the enemy facing him was probably considerably lower than that of the professional Seleucid army whom he later fought. Thus their stability in battle, particularly under the detrimental conditions Judas forced upon them, certainly reduced their ability or desire to withstand the Maccabean attacks.

Defeat of Seron

As with Apollonius, the second attempt to destroy Judas' growing guerrilla army was a unilateral decision by Seron, a middle-ranking Seleucid official, determined to lead a successful expedition and so gain kudos in the eyes of his superiors. The clear inference is that neither the officials in Jerusalem nor Antiochus himself took the threat of Judas seriously, or had heard of him as yet. It would seem that the Seleucid force moved southwards from Seron's base in Coele-Syria, approximately to southern Phoenicia, following the coastal route and then swung inland through Judaea. They intended to march through the pass at Beth-Horon, one of the traditional invasion routes into the Judaean hills, but it was here that Judas decided to attack.

There were, in fact, two places of that name: one a 'Lower' and the other an 'Upper' Beth-Horon located at the top of the pass. The place was one of some pedigree in the history of the Jewish people for it was in

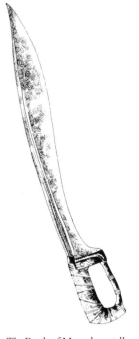

The Book of Maccabees tells how Judas took the sword from the body of Apollonius and wore it throughout his life. The kopis, a single-edged slashing sword, was popular throughout the Greco–Roman world at this time. One belonging to a superior officer such as Apollonius would have been ornate and personalised.

159

The Army Advances

To command the army, Lysias chose Ptolemy, a professional soldier and general in charge of Seleucid forces in Coele-Syria and Phoenicia; but he devolved the leadership of the actual campaign to Nicanor, son of Patroclus, who was one of the King's 'Close Friends'. He in turn appointed an experienced general by the name of Gorgias to command the army. Obviously a man after the King's heart, Nicanor suggested raising tribute by the sale of Jewish prisoners of war. He lost no time in sending to the seaboard towns an invitation to come and buy Jewish manpower.

The size of the Seleucid army that the *First Book of Maccabees* (3:39) speaks of as advancing on Judaea is plainly in error, a result of the common tendency of ancient writers to exaggerate. Thus we are presented with the claim that Lysias 'despatched forty thousand foot and seven thousand cavalry to invade the land of Judah'. Whereas in the *Second Book of Maccabees* (8:9) the writer speaks of a smaller force comprising at least twenty thousand men.

Whilst other figures given in the *Second Book of Maccabees* for the forces engaged in battles are greatly exaggerated, the figure of at least 20,000 men is reasonable in this case. Certainly, Bar Kochva in his study of the Seleucid army thinks that a figure in excess of 20,000 men, including locally recruited Edomaean and Philistine mercenary auxiliaries, is likely. The much larger figure given in the *First Book of Maccabees* and quoted above means that such a force would have comprised the bulk of the army Antiochus displayed at Daphne in 166 B.C. (46,000 foot

It was along the pass separating the two settlements of Lower Beth-Horon (above) and Upper Beth-Horon that Judas triumphed over Seron's Seleucid forces. Catching them strung out over the length of the pass, his attack on the head of the enemy column produced panic and fear down its entire length. There were many Seleucid casualties.

After defeating Lysias at Beth-Zur, Judas returned to Jerusalem, where in December 164 B.C. the Temple was cleansed and rededicated with great jubilation. The event is celebrated to this day in the Festival of Hanukkah.

soldiers, including a Macedonian phalanx of 20,000 men, 8,500 cavalry and 36 or 42 elephants). But as we have already stated, the main elements of this army were ear-marked by Antiochus for the much more important campaign against the Parthians. Thus, the writer of the *First Book of Maccabees* cannot be correct in suggesting that Antiochus left half of his troops to deal with the Jewish rebellion. It is simply a case of the official historian of the House of Hasmon exaggerating numbers in order to show Judas Maccabeus in an even more favourable light.

When the news of the size of this Seleucid force reached Judaea, together with information about their intentions towards the Jewish population, there was understandable trepidation. Even Judas and his brothers saw the situation as going from bad to worse.

The Seleucid army, having advanced southwards, encamped at Emmaus and being, it seems, in no hurry, proceeded to hold 'court' as the local merchants arrived at the camp, bringing with them a large amount of gold and silver, as well as proposing to buy the Israelites as slaves. Perhaps the very arrogance and over-confidence implied by this event helps to explain the subsequent Seleucid defeat.

The Battle of Emmaus

Judas was aware of the strength of the army marching to 'destroy' him as he would have had it under observation as soon as it approached Judaea. However, the army of Nicanor faced him with a situation he had not yet had to confront – the need to give battle with a large, well-equipped and very powerful Seleucid army. Furthermore, the knowledge 'that the King had ordered the people's total destruction' weighed heavily on the choices open to Judas. Doubtless he was fully aware of the capacity for such a force to engage in a long campaign against him, particularly if the ruthless policy of exterminating the population destroyed the very intelligence, supply and support base on which his guerrilla army depended. Whether he liked it or not, he would have to move against the Seleucid army at the earliest possible opportunity.

Given the mood of the times and the great threat bearing down upon them the people gathered at Mizpah, the traditional rallying place of the people of Israel. There they called on the Lord for mercy and attempted to divine his will with respect to the forthcoming battle.

Again the *Books of Maccabees* are in disagreement as to the size of the force that Judas took against the Seleucids. However, we can presume that Judas was able to bring to battle at least 3000 men and perhaps as many as 6000. Whilst preferring to depend on his own guerrilla forces, on the grounds of their reliability, the size of the enemy he was up against no doubt dictated the need to impress as many men as he could into the army he was to take into the field. He must have been acutely conscious of the disparity between his own force and that of the enemy in terms not only of weaponry and equipment but also of his men's lack of experience

Maccabean infantry at Emmaus would have looked little different than when the revolt started – apart from the growing effectiveness of weapons obtained mainly from those abandoned by the Seleucids.

in open warfare. So whilst he needed numbers, he also needed a plan that would allow him to exploit his traditional guerrilla strengths of knowledge of terrain, stealth and surprise. He therefore decided to attack the Seleucid forces at Emmaus without delay.

Forming up his men, he moved northwards and took up a position some miles to the south of the Seleucid encampment at Emmaus. However, unlike his opponents in their 'settlement' of tents and large baggage train, Judas required his men to stand to arms with only a few fires to mark their presence.

It would seem then that Judas had originally intended to fight a conventional battle against the Seleucid army on the following day and that the prospects for a successful outcome were not at all promising. However, during the night something occurred that swung the whole issue in his favour. Word came back to him – no doubt from men he had detached to observe the enemy encampment – that a large force had detached itself from the main body and was heading towards Judas' encampment.

Indeed this was the case. Gorgias had decided to fall on Judas while still in his camp (clearly his position was known!) and had told Nicanor that

It was in the vicinity of Emmaus – as it appears today – that Judas Maccabeus and his army was able to inflict their first defeat on a regular Seleucid army that had been raised to destroy the rebels and suppress the Jewish rebellion.

163

he was taking 5000 foot and 1000 cavalry in order to do so. At the dead of night and led by Jewish sympathisers, the Seleucid force made their way, probably slowly on account of their unfamiliarity with and the roughness of the terrain, towards where they knew Judas to be. With a headstart, Judas struck his own camp and, leading his men rapidly over ground they knew like the back of their hand, made straight for the Seleucid encampment at Emmaus. He assumed that those in the encampment would imagine that Gorgias would rapidly destroy the Jewish forces and that they needed no assistance to do so, secure in the belief that this Jewish thorn in the flesh was even now being destroyed.

Even as Gorgias arrived at Judas' abandoned camp, and jumped to the erroneous conclusion that the Jews had withdrawn rather than fight, the Maccabean forces were drawn up in front of the Seleucid encampment at Emmaus, ready for battle.

By now it was first light and Judas was too wily a commander not to take advantage of the lowered guard and slowness of response that come with waking from sleep. With an encampment only half-awake and secure in the false knowledge that its enemy was even now being destroyed, Judas ordered the trumpets to be blown and the advance began. Panic enveloped the Seleucid camp and even though some forces managed to deploy to face the rapidly advancing Jewish line, it was to no avail. The Maccabean forces swept in and, caught totally off guard, the Seleucid forces dissolved in front of the ferocious onslaught. Fleeing for their lives, the retreat became a rout.

Victory

Judas instructed his well disciplined forces to halt the pursuit:

'Never mind the booty, for we have another battle ahead of us. First stand up to our enemies and fight them and then you can safely collect the booty'. The words were hardly out of Judas' mouth, when a detachment came into view, peering down from the mountain. Observing that their own troops had been routed and that the camp had been fired – since the smoke, which they could see attested the fact – they were panic stricken at the sight; and when, furthermore they saw Judas' troops drawn up for battle on the plain, they all fled into Philistine territory. Judas then turned back to plunder the camp, and a large sum in gold and silver, with violet and sea purple stuffs and other valuables were carried off.

(1 *Maccabees* 4:18–24)

Judas had won a remarkable victory, realised through great daring and audacity. However, the Seleucids were not about to give up their hold on Judaea and within a short time of their defeat at Emmaus they were putting together another army to destroy Judas. This time, however, the campaign was to be led and waged by Lysias himself, so alarmed had he become about the passage of events in Judaea.

At the same time, it was the make up of the opposing armies and the tactics employed that had contributed to the victories of Judas – and which was to influence the outcome of his greatest battles.

Armies and Weapons

In the six years between his assumption of the leadership of the Jewish resistance forces and his death at the battle of Elasa in 160 B.C., Judas Maccabeus was involved in almost continual warfare with the forces of the Seleucid empire. Over that period the Maccabean forces evolved from their origins as a guerrilla force into an army able to take on their Seleucid opponents in conventional battle. The Book of Maccabees constantly portrays Judas as the underdog, with small forces. This is a result of the historian of the House of Hasmon not wanting to diminish the scale or glory of the victories – and to provide an excuse for defeats. In reality there is evidence to show that the numbers of men available between 166 and 160 B.C. were considerably larger than those suggested, particularly after the re-dedication of the Temple in 164 B.C.

The Growing Army

In the early days of the rebellion the numbers of men available were very small although these rapidly grew in number as the fame of Judas spread. By the Battle of Emmaus in 164 B.C., some two years after the beginning of the rebellion, Judas was able to put 3000 men into the field.

However, the greatest increase in the size of the Maccabean army occurred after the purification of the Temple. In the expeditions into the regions around Judaea to bring back those Jews lying beyond the protection of his arms he could field at least 20,000 men, such a figure being arrived at by totalling the men despatched on the various expeditions to the areas surrounding Judaea as well as those lost in battle. The biblical image of continually small Maccabean forces taking on overwhelmingly large enemy armies and overcoming them is just not tenable.

Maccabean Weaponry

Throughout the time that Judas led the rebels the bulk of his forces were light infantry. In the early days, when functioning in a guerrilla capacity, the Maccabean forces were poorly equipped, with many of the better weapons and other equipment such as body armour being obtained as booty from the defeated Seleucid forces, just as Judas acquired his own sword from the hand of the dead Apollonius. However, by the time of Beth-Zechariah, when Judas was able to oppose the Seleucid phalanx with one of his own, the equipment would have been manufactured in the towns of Judaea as well as being brought into the province by the Jews returning from abroad.

The nearly continuous warfare in which Judas was involved, particularly after 164 B.C., must point to more sophisticated means of weapons acquisition, although the Maccabean forces on the battlefield would never have looked like the regular units of the Seleucid army. Apart from

Almost all the helmets employed by the Seleucid soldiery were variations of the Thracian type. Whilst those of officers were sometimes of iron, those of the other ranks were normally made of bronze, either left in the natural metal finish or painted.

the heavy infantry, most of the lighter units would have eschewed a uniform and retained the appearance of 'organised irregulars'. From the account in the *First Book of Maccabees* of Judas mustering his forces prior to the battle of Emmaus, the Maccabean organisation seems to have been in the traditional form, from Moses, of units of 1000 subdivided into hundreds, fifties and tens. While the text makes no mention of the Maccabean forces possessing cavalry, there is an interesting 'slip of the pen' in the *Second Book of Maccabees* in which there is mention of a horseman called Dositheus. Bar-Kochva, the eminent authority on the Seleucid army, believes that he can show fairly conclusively that Dositheus came from a Ptolemaic military settlement in the Trans-Jordan.

The Seleucid Phalanx

The core of the Seleucid armies of Antiochus IV Epiphanes, of Demetrius and of all other Seleucid monarchs, in keeping with the Hellenistic tradition in warfare, was the phalanx. Throughout the greater period of the existence of the Empire, the Seleucid kings were able to deploy on the major campaigns two corps of phalangites or phalanx troopers numbering 'some tens of thousands'. These two corps were designated either simply the 'phalanx' or the argyraspides, who were the infantry guard. These were available as a permanent force at the heart of the Empire. Whilst predominantly encountered as part of the Seleucid phalanx, the argyraspides were also employed as non-phalanx infantry, suggesting a capacity to change rôle as needs demanded.

In the light of the central role played by the phalanx, and of the heterogeneity of peoples within the Seleucid empire, it was vital for the kings to be able to draw on a large number of loyal persons to serve within the phalanx. It is not surprising therefore to discover that such troops were exclusively recruited from the ranks of military settlers living in settlements known as *katoikiai*, established by the Seleucids to provide them with a steady source of able and loyal manpower. The inhabitants of these *katoikiai*, of which there were some forty-five, were predominantly Greco-Macedonians, their descendants holding land from the King in return for the obligation to provide military service. This was a generational compact in which the sons of soldiers inherited the obligations to serve along with the land. This enabled the Seleucid kings to maintain a phalanx stable in numbers for some considerable time, even taking into account losses on campaign.

The hard core of the phalangist infantry was concentrated in settlements close to the heart of the empire around Antioch in northern Syria to allow rapid mobilisation in time of war. Such settlements also provided the horse guard and the cataphracts, and possibly some light cavalry as well. From the *katoikiai* in Asia Minor, northern Syria and Mesopotamia and the eastern provinces, of which Media was the most important, it seems that some 44,000 phalangists, 3000 semi-heavy

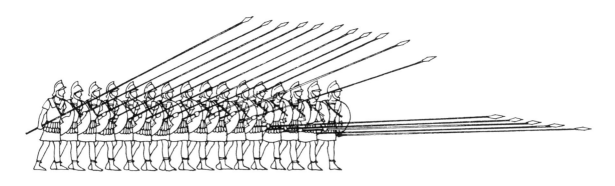

infantry and 8000–8500 cavalry could be raised. This marked the maximum recruitment potential rather than the actual forces deployed. At Magnesia, for example, the infantry from the settlements allowed a phalanx of 16,000 men to be deployed. However, as the Seleucid borders contracted and military settlements were lost, the numbers available for service declined.

Infantry in Action

The phalanx of Antiochus Epiphanes was, in many respects, identical to that of his predecessors but with his own innovations. Composed of chrysaspides, chalkaspides and the argyraspides, all phalangists were equipped with the huge, two-handed pike – the 7 metre-long sarissa. The shield, some 45 cm in diameter, was strapped to the left forearm allowing the 6 kilogramme sarissa to be held in both hands on the right side of the body.

The name argyraspides, meaning 'silver shields', went back to the time when Alexander issued silver shields to his hypaspists before the great battle of the Hydaspes in India. They formed a unit that retained its size at 10,000 men, recruited again from the *katoikiai* but from amongst the fittest and most able in the empire. Under Antiochus, some 5000 of the argyraspides had their traditional Macedonian panoply of heavy body armour and greaves replaced by a new uniform and equipment in the manner of the Roman triarius, except for the traditional helmet which was retained. The King hoped that by employing the more flexible Roman 'infantry' alongside the power of the phalanx he could exploit the strengths of both to his advantage. Indeed, at Beth-Zechariah it was the 'Roman' units with their mail armour who were detailed to protect the elephants in the first division moving into the defile against the Maccabean phalanx.

Apart from the phalangists, other Seleucid infantry included numbers of peltasts or thureophoroi. However, many of these troops were also recruited as mercenaries and as many as 10,000 may have served on Antiochus' expedition against the Parthians. Certainly, the Seleucids made extensive use of infantry recruited locally. These troops tended to

Little is known of the tactical organisation of the Seleucid phalanx, the core of the professional Seleucid army, though this is its probable general appearance. However, by the time of the Jewish rebellion, bitter experience at the hands of the more flexible tactical organisation of the Roman Legion meant that on the battlefield the days of the phalanx were numbered.

The phalangites, carrying their 21-foot sarissas and their shields strapped to their left arms, formed the main striking units of the field armies.

be poorly trained and poorly motivated and were just used to bolster the numbers of the field army, as at Magnesia.

Cataphracts

We have already mentioned that the regular cavalry were recruited from the military settlements. By the time of Magnesia, all the cavalry – other than the two élite guard units which numbered 1000 men – were of the heavy type known as cataphracts. The first élite cavalry unit was named 'the Companions' and was recruited from the settlements in Lydia, Syria and Phrygia. The second unit, or the Agema, was originally recruited from amongst the Medes until the area succumbed to the Parthians, after which a new Agema was recruited from the 'Macedonian' colonists. Unlike the regular cavalry, the élite units were not equipped as full cataphracts. They were described by Livy at Magnesia as having 'lighter protection for their riders and their mounts, but in other equipment not unlike the cataphracts'. The movement towards a heavy cavalry arm came in the wake of Antiochus III's experiences fighting the Parthians. They made such an impression that by the time of the Battle of Magnesia all the cavalry had been re-equipped as such. The Greek historian Polybius described their appearance as 'men and horses completely armoured'.

Elephants of War

However, the Seleucids were most famous for their use of elephants. Although by the beginning of the reign of Antiochus III only ten elephants remained from a once large herd, through trade he was able to raise the figure to 102 by 217 B.C. With additional animals secured from

Bactrian and Indian sources he was able to further increase his herd to 150. Once again, by the time of Antiochus IV the number of elephants had been drastically reduced. However, despite the treaty of Apamea, which required all elephants to be handed over to the Romans, the King still managed to take an undetermined number on his Egyptian campaign. At Daphne in 166 B.C. he paraded either 36 or 42 elephants, which probably represented the total herd available to him. Indeed, the last time that the Seleucids were to use elephants on a field of battle was during Lysias' second campaign against Judas and in the Battle of Beth-Zechariah – the appearance of the elephants probably being the determining factor in the battle, so unused were Judas' men to fighting against such creatures. In all, Lysias probably only had about eight available to him.

It is not possible to do more than sketch the make-up of the military forces of the respective combatants of this time but it was with these

Though for so long the distinctive feature of the Seleucid field armies, Beth-Zechariah marked the last occasion that the war elephant was employed by the Seleucids. Nevertheless, these animals, albeit extensively protected by shielding units, did much to shatter the Maccabean line in that battle.

Beth-Zur was strategically sited in this dramatic landscape alongside the southern route to Jerusalem. On his second campaign in 162 B.C., the Seleucid commander Lysias discovered that Judas Maccabeus had fortified and garrisoned the settlement. The need to protect his lines of communications required that Lysias capture the place.

forces that Maccabee and Seleucid set out to determine the fate of Judaea and the Jewish people.

Victory at Beth-Zur

In the wake of the débâcle at Emmaus, Lysias must have realised that in the person of Judas he was faced with an enemy of no mean military ability. Furthermore, his own standing and even his life may well now be in the balance once the news of Emmaus reached the ears of the King. Having decided that the only politic thing to do was to re-establish his credibility by ending the Jewish rebellion once and for all, he set about raising another army with the intention of leading the next campaign to Judaea himself.

In the short account of the first campaign of Lysias (1 *Maccabees* 4:28ff), we are faced with a description of a Seleucid army that is much too large given the forces actually available. Lysias is described as having mobilised 60,000 picked troops and 5000 cavalry with the intention

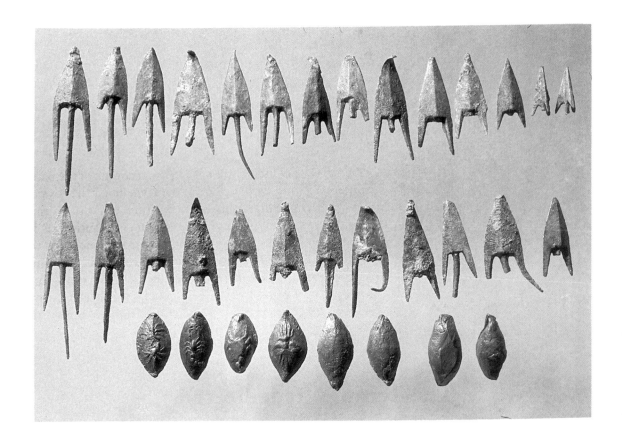

of finishing off the Jews. In the *Second Book of Maccabees* (11:2) we are presented with even larger figures – some 80,000 foot soldiers and Lysias' entire cavalry. The difficulty with either set of figures is that at this time – that is before the death of Antiochus IV – the bulk of the forces available to the Seleucids as a whole were engaged in the campaign in the east against the Parthians.

Although excavated at Acco, these Hellenistic arrowheads and slings are typical of the projectile weapons used against the defenders of Beth-Zur.

Key to Jerusalem

With his army assembled, Lysias advanced on Judaea. Learning from the lessons of the previous expeditions he deliberately avoided the obvious line of advance, which was to climb onto the Judaean plateau by way of the north or north-western passes. He was fully aware of the degree to which the Jewish population in those regions was hostile to the Seleucids, and he had no desire to present Judas with another opportunity to catch a Seleucid army strung out and vulnerable in a mountain pass. He therefore took his army by the south-western route, which allowed him to approach Jerusalem from the south after passing through the territory of the Edomaeans, who supported the Seleucids against the Jews. Both sides were aware that the key to Jerusalem was the fortress of

171

Beth-Zur, lying some 27 kilometres to the south of the city, and it was there that Judas had assembled his force of 10,000 men.

By all the accounts of the subsequent battle, Judas managed to defeat Lysias:

the two forces engaged, and five thousand men of Lysias' troops fell in hand to hand fighting. Seeing the rout of his army and the courage of Judas' and their readiness to live or die nobly, Lysias withdrew to Antioch.

(1 *Maccabees* 4:34–35)

Now, it is possible, given the inconsistencies in the accounts of the battle in both *Books of Maccabees* and by Josephus in the *Antiquities*, that Lysias' abandonment of the battlefield and his sudden return to Antioch may have had more to do with receiving news of the illness of Antiochus IV Epiphanes on campaign in the east. The political consequences for the succession would have been considered serious enough, with as much threat to his own position as from the results of the Battle of Beth-Zur.

For Judas, however, the abandonment of Judaea by the Seleucid army meant that the Jews could now realise their ambition to purify the Temple and re-dedicate the sanctuary in Jerusalem.

The Temple Rededicated

In the wake of Lysias' defeat at Beth-Zur, Judas determined to seize the initiative and return to Jerusalem to purge it of the pro-Seleucid and apostate Jews and purify and re-dedicate the Temple of the Lord.

With his army in tow, Judas entered the holy city and went up to Mount Zion on which stood the 'Temple'. They found the sanctuary deserted, the altar desecrated, the gates burned down, and vegetation growing in the courtyards.

Despite the dismay and anger at what he found, Judas was determined to rectify the situation. With the pro-Seleucid party effectively holed up in the Akra, he selected priests who had shown no taint of Hellenism and who were 'blameless and zealous for the Law' to begin the task of purifying the sanctuary. The act of the greatest profanity and pollution in the holiest of places was the erection of the altar to Olympian Zeus on the order of Antiochus. The altar was demolished and the stones placed in a cave on the hill of the Dwelling. The priests:

took unhewn stones, as the Law prescribed, and built a new altar on the lines of the old one. They restored the Holy Place and the interior of the Dwelling, and purified the courts. They made new sacred vessels, and brought the lamp stand, the altar of incense and the table into the Temple. They burned incense on the altar and lit the lamps on the lamp stand and these shone inside the Temple. They placed the loaves on the table and hung the curtains and completed all the tasks they had undertaken.

(1 *Maccabees* 4:47–51)

Festival of Lights

So it was that on the 25th of the month of Chislev (December 164 B.C.) and on the third anniversary of the first sacrifice to Zeus the priests 'offered a Lawful sacrifice of burnt offering which they had made'. Then there followed eight days of celebration and festivities, the disgrace inflicted by the Seleucids having been finally effaced.

As a consequence of this event:

> Judas, with his brothers and the whole assembly of Israel made it a law that the days of dedication of the altar should be celebrated yearly at the proper season, for eight days beginning on the twenty fifth of the month Chislev, with rejoicing and gladness.
>
> (1 Maccabees 4:59)

The seven-branched candlestick called the Menorah is still used each year to commemorate Hanukkah, the Festival of Lights.

This festival is still commemorated to this day and is known in the Jewish religious calendar as The Festival of Lights or Hanukkah. In many Jewish homes, the seven-branched candlestick known as the Menorah is lit, with one candle being lit for each day of the festival. Thus the Jews of the present day keep faith with their ancestors who fought so desperately to keep their faith alive in the face of a ruthless and vindictive attempt to destroy it – truly a victory of light over darkness.

End of an Enemy

The death of Antiochus IV Epiphanes in late 164 B.C., at the time of the re-dedication of the Temple, was seen as the judgement of God on the arrogance and cruelty of this man, who had presumed to call himself a 'god' and had polluted the Temple of the Lord:

> And so this murderer and blasphemer, having endured sufferings as terrible as those which he had made others endure, met his pitiable fate, and ended his life in the mountains far from his home
>
> (2 Maccabees 9:28)

Judas followed up the death of his enemy and of the purification of the sanctuary by fortifying the Temple Mount and the strategic site of Beth-Zur. He had every reason to suppose that Lysias would return at the head of a larger army and resume the attempt to crush the revolt.

At the same time with the majority of the Seleucid forces out of Judaea, Judas took the opportunity to strike out at those in the surrounding territories who had exploited the edict of Antiochus by attacking Jews outside Judaea. Leading his armies out beyond the borders of the province for the first time, he fought successfully against the Edomaeans in the south, the 'children of Baean' and the Ammonites. This prompted the populations in Gilead and the Trans-Jordan to persecute any Jews in those areas, so Judas delegated Simon to lead a force into Galilee. Having defeated the enemy there, Simon led the Jewish families of Galilee and Arbatta and their possessions to Judaea in triumph.

An attempt to take Jamnia was defeated by the Seleucid general Gorgias, but during a second campaign against the Edomites Judas took

The Edomaeans, against whom Judas also campaigned, were more than happy to allow the Seleucid armies transit through their territory and supplied Lysias with many auxiliary troops to attack Judaea from the south.

the ancient city of Hebron where David had once ruled as King. Pushing into the coastal plain, Judas destroyed the temples of the former Philistine city of Ashdod. With the surrounding areas pacified, he returned to Jerusalem determined to destroy forever the renegades from amongst his own people even now walled up behind the great defences of the citadel, the Akra (or Acra), on the Temple Mount.

Battle of Beth-Zechariah

It was in the winter of 163–162 B.C. that Judas began the siege of the Akra in Jerusalem. Bringing siege engines to back up the blockade, they attempted to break through the very powerful defences of the Akra, but to little avail. This was a telling tribute to the sophisticated design of Seleucid fortifications. It was also a comment on the lack of skill and expertise possessed by the Maccabean forces when it came to siege techniques.

The blockade was also not secure enough to prevent a few of the besieged from escaping. With the help of a number of renegades, these pro-Seleucids made their way to Antioch to petition Antiochus V to come to their aid.

In reality their appeal was not so much to the King – who was only nine years of age – but to Lysias who, having declared himself Regent, was the real power in the land. Lysias certainly had no desire to write off Judaea and there can be no doubting that his initial defeat by Judas at Beth-Zur still rankled. The Seleucid court was always a place of intrigue and it was important that Lysias demonstrate his power and recover his prestige. Settling finally with Judas and his 'Maccabean' rebels offered the obvious opportunity. Lysias thus once more set about the task of raising an army and one that this time would be unlikely to be bettered by the wily Jewish rebel.

The Forces Gather

Despite the two conflicting accounts of a total for the Seleucid army of 'a hundred thousand foot soldiers, twenty thousand cavalry and thirty two elephants' (1 *Maccabees* 6:30) and 'one hundred and ten thousand infantry, five thousand cavalry, twenty two elephants and three hundred chariots fitted with scythes' (2 *Maccabees* 13:2), a figure in the region of 50,000 infantry and 5000 cavalry, including many Edomaean and Phoenician mercenaries, is probably nearer the truth. This is supported by the historian Bar-Kochva, who also argues for a total of about eight elephants (this being the last occasion they were employed by the Seleucids) and for no chariots to have taken part at all. As he did during his first campaign, Lysias approached Judaea from the south-west

The most common of the Edomaean auxiliaries were archers. Very lightly armed, apart from the compound bow, they provided the Seleucids with valuable longer range fire support.

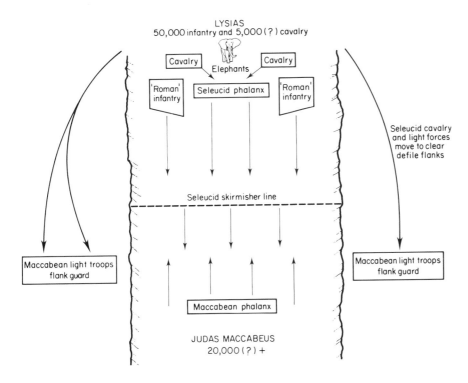

Probable disposition of the Seleucid and Maccabean forces in the defile at Beth-Zechariah, just prior to the initial clash of arms.

combatants, as well as its mahout. The remainder of the cavalry was stationed on one or other of the two flanks of the army, to harass the enemy and cover the phalanxes.

(1 *Maccabees* 6:35–38)

In his *Jewish Antiquities* Flavius Josephus speaks of these 'self-contained units' deploying from a wide battle line into column before entering the defile to confront the Maccabean forces. Thus each unit presented to the enemy what was in itself a miniature of the battle line.

Gallantry in Defeat

From the description given in *Maccabees*, the phalanxes were equipped not with the more usual phalangites but with soldiers dressed and equipped in the Roman fashion, allowing them to respond more flexibly in the confined spaces of the defile. Screened by a line of skirmishers, the Seleucid line advanced towards the Jewish forces. It was at this point that, according to *Maccabees*, one 'Eleazar called Avran', the brother of Judas, launched himself forward into the Seleucid troops and, having cut his way through, attacked an elephant believing it to be carrying the boy King. Whilst making for good reading, the whole event is most unlikely to have occurred in the manner described, simply on the grounds that

Lured away from the main battle at Elasa by a Seleucid stratagem, Judas and his small cavalry force were isolated and cut off by Bacchides' guards. So died the great hero, beneath the enemy lances, in 160 B.C.

one man would hardly have been able to cut through so many enemy soldiers who were there specifically to protect the elephants. Nevertheless, it is very probable that there was an outstanding deed of courage by a single Jewish soldier to inspire his comrades in the face of growing defeat.

The Bible has very little to say about the course of this very important battle, perhaps because in the end it was a severe defeat for Judas and his army. It is difficult to speculate with so little evidence, but a plausible scenario is that the Seleucid forces on the hills rapidly pushed aside the Jewish units covering the flanks of the defile and exposed the Maccabean forces in the defile itself. Under growing and powerful frontal pressure in the defile itself, with the elephants generating a deep sense of unease and fear, the limited success the Maccabeans had achieved in the centre against the Seleucid skirmishers gave way. Their flanks now exposed and the enemy cavalry pushing into their rear, panic set in and the Maccabean army fled from the field, abandoning most of their equipment and leaving behind many dead and dying. Such must be inferred from the silence of the text on this matter. From Josephus we learn that, having abandoned the battlefield, Judas and his surviving followers fled to Gophna, into the hills near Bethel. The scale of the Jewish defeat now unlocked the door to Jerusalem and once again it looked to Judas that the Holy City and the Temple, so recently purified and re-dedicated was to be polluted by the presence of the gentiles.

Religious Freedom

As the news of the disastrous defeat of Judas at Beth-Zechariah reached Jerusalem, only the pro-Seleucid forces still blockaded in the Akra gave thanks. For the rest of the population, it seemed that their nemesis was coming closer with every mile that Lysias' army drew nearer the city. Many of the soldiers that survived the defeat set about preparing the city for the inevitable siege that was to follow.

With the fortress of Beth-Zur now under his control and garrisoned, Lysias could bring up the machines that formed so formidable an element in the Seleucid arsenal:

He besieged the sanctuary for a long time, erecting battering and siege engines, flame throwers and ballistas, scorpions to discharge arrows and catapults. The defenders countered these by constructing their own engines and were thus able to prolong their own resistance.

(1 *Maccabees* 6:51–53)

However, there was virtually no food in the city and starvation began to take its toll. As it was the seventh year, the 'Sabbatical Rest' in which no crops were sown, it was not possible to lay in reserves in the food stores.

Very large numbers of light skirmishing troops, like this thurephoros or peltast, were used by the Seleucids. They preceded the phalanx into battle, dispatching their javelins to unnerve and unsteady the enemy line. At Beth-Zechariah, the only Maccabean success lay in their defeat of the Seleucid skirmisher line.

Food shortages also affected the attackers, for there were no crops for them either, and what little there was was hidden by the hostile populace. Thus when Lysias received news that Philip – whom Antiochus Epiphanes had appointed before his death to act as Regent to his son – had returned to Antioch and was even now moving to assume power in the empire, he resolved to end the siege and the war post haste and return to Syria to protect his position.

Murder of the High Priest

In the name of the King, Lysias offered peace to the Jews on the basis of a return to the law granting them the right to freedom of worship as laid down by Antiochus III.

However, to the Seleucids the offer covered only the Temple and not the city walls, which they felt at liberty to pull down. Having retained their political authority over Judaea, it was clearly expedient to destroy the means whereby the city could hold out against them if ever the need arose in the future to quell rebellion in the province. According to Josephus, amongst the baggage and booty taken by the Seleucids when they returned to Antioch was Menelaus, the High Priest. He was put to death on the order of Antiochus V by being thrown down into a tower full of ashes, the King having been told by Lysias that Menelaus was responsible for the Seleucid woes in Judaea.

New King and New Priest

In 162 B.C. Demetrius, grandson of Antiochus III and rightful heir to the Seleucid throne, managed to escape from an enforced Roman custody with the assistance of the Greek historian and statesman Polybius. He made his way to Antioch where he was successful in wooing the army to his cause as the rightful king of the Seleucid empire. That same year he was crowned, taking the name Demetrius I Soter (Preserver).

It was the revolt against him by the Seleucid general Timarchus in Babylonia and the subsequent drawing eastwards of the bulk of Demetrius' main army to deal with the revolt that provided Judas with the opportunity to make a final bid for political freedom of his people.

Many Jews were prepared to forgo any further opposition to the Seleucid crown on the grounds that they had been granted full religious freedom. However, Judas Maccabeus felt that the Jews could never be certain that freedom to live according to their ancestral Law would not be rescinded again, unless they were politically independent of any foreign power.

Not surprisingly, a political struggle began in Judea between those who supported the Seleucids, and the others, led by Judas, who wished to continue the fight for full political independence. Naturally the Seleucids had no reason or desire to deal with Judas, and so consciously set about strengthening the Hellenising party amongst the Jews.

In 162 B.C. Demetrius, son of Seleucus IV, escaped from Rome. Returning to Antioch he procured the deaths of Lysias and Antiochus V with the help of the army. In 160 B.C., he despatched an army to Judaea under Bacchides with instructions to kill Judas Maccabeus.

When Demetrius became King in Antioch he appointed in Jerusalem a new High Priest by the name of Alcimus. Whilst Alcimus was a member of a legitimate priestly family, he was also a Helleniser. This provoked the wrath of Judas, who managed to prevent him taking up his post in Jerusalem. After appealing to the King in Antioch, Alcimus was sent back to Jerusalem escorted by an army under the generalship of Bacchides. Attempts to parley with the Maccabean forces came to nought, but on the road to Jerusalem an incident occurred that transformed the situation:

> A commission of scribes presented themselves before Alcimus and Bacchides, to sue for just terms. The first among the Israelites to ask for peace terms were the Hasidaeans who reasoned thus, 'This is a priest of Aaron's line who has come with the armed forces; he will not wrong us.' He did in fact discuss peace terms with them and gave them his oath, 'We shall not attempt to injure you and your friends'. They believed him, but he arrested sixty of them and put them to death.
>
> (1 *Maccabees* 7:12–16)

Why such an action occurred is difficult to fathom. Perhaps in this crude way Alcimus was demonstrating that he would brook no challenge to his authority. If so, it was a lamentable error.

Defeat of Nicanor

The Hasidaeans had supported Judas throughout the fight for religious freedom and had only broken with him once it was realised. Now they saw that it was not possible for their religious convictions to be reconciled with the new High Priest and the Seleucid King who supported him.

The situation disintegrated rapidly. The Hasidaeans returned to serve with Judas and he resorted to purging the countryside of any avowed supporters of the Hellenising party.

In the place of Bacchides, Demetrius sent Nicanor, who as 'one of his generals ranking as illustrious and bitter enemy of Israel' (1 *Maccabees* 7:26), brought an army to Judaea with orders to exterminate the people.

An attempt to abduct Judas failed. Judas called out his army and the Maccabean and Seleucid forces met on the battlefield of Adasa, where Nicanor was defeated and his army virtually destroyed. Having collected the spoils and booty, Judas' men cut off Nicanor's head and his right hand, which he had stretched out in a display of insolence. These gory trophies were taken and displayed within sight of Jerusalem, to the people's great acclaim.

Roman Treaty

In the brief period of peace that followed, Judas demonstrated his political acumen by entering into negotiations with the Romans to conclude a treaty. It is clear to see his thinking: if the Romans guaranteed Judaean independence, then the Seleucids would not dare to invade.

Within the context of Roman interests, such a policy was also quite advantageous. A treaty with Judaea would severely limit Seleucid power in the area – always a matter to their liking – and further divide the territory. In addition, the relationship would see Judas placed in a position of dependence on Rome.

The terms of the treaty are worth quoting:

> If war comes first to Rome or any of her allies throughout her dominions the Jewish nation will take action as her ally, as occasion may require, and do it wholeheartedly. . . . In the same way, if war comes first to the Jewish nation, the Romans will support them energetically as occasion may offer.

Most important of all for Judas was the following clause that he felt must have assured the Jews of both their political as well as their religious freedom:

> As regards the wrongs done to them by King Demetrius we have written to him in these terms: Why have you made your yoke lie heavy on our friends and allies the Jews? If they appeal against you again, we shall uphold their rights and make war on you by sea and land.

> (1 *Maccabees* 8:24–32)

In the light of this treaty it must have been a surprise for Judas to learn that a Seleucid plan was afoot to 'seek out and finally destroy this meddlesome and perverse Jewish rebel'.

Death at Elasa

Demetrius had suppressed the Babylonian revolt of Timarchus and was now in a position to make available a large and powerful force with which to deal once and for all with Judas Maccabeus, the treaty between the Romans and the Jews notwithstanding. Believing that only by striking quickly could the problem in Judaea be solved, Demetrius summoned Bacchides to plan a strategy. For the first time the explicit objective was the full elimination of the leaders of the Jewish revolt. The intention was to paralyse the body by severing the head.

Whilst such an approach was certainly logical, Judas Maccabeus had never obliged the Seleucids by dancing to their battle tune unless absolutely necessary; Bacchides knew that he would have to draw Judas and his army out to fight on a battlefield of his choosing. The Seleucid strategos therefore selected with care not only his line of march into Judaea – eschewing all previous well trodden and familiar paths – but also the site of the battle and the tactics employed on the battlefield itself.

The lighter Maccabean cavalry as it was probably equipped at Elasa. Judas Maccabeus rode in the cavalry in the battle but would have been more extensively armoured.

New Tactics

In previous campaigns Seleucid forces had attempted to reach the

Judaean plateau either by approaching via the passes in the northern part of the province – in which case Judas had ambushed them as in the 'battles' against Apollonius and Seron – or they had approached from the south-west, having first attempted to seize the strategically placed fortress of Beth-Zur, and then marched on Jerusalem as Lysias had done some two years previously. Bacchides reasoned that it was likely that Judas would expect him to do the same. He therefore planned 'a strategy of the indirect approach', hoping to place himself and his army on the plateau before Judas realised what was happening. This is indeed what actually happened. Marshalling his army – reported in the *First Book of Maccabees* at 20,000 infantry and 2000 cavalry, figures with which Bar-Kochva generally concurs, including at most 10,000 phalangites to form a large phalanx – Bacchides took a route to the south-east. This allowed him to enter Judaea by the very difficult and tortuous path from the Jordan valley onto the plateau using an ascent that, although 21 kilometres long, allowed him to debouch his army in one piece and safe onto the plateau in less than a day's march. This strategem totally outwitted Judas who was unable to act quickly enough. Judas' failure to anticipate this move was largely due to lack of intelligence: the line of march taken by the Seleucid strategos had the added advantage of moving through sparsely settled Jewish territory with very few eyes and ears with which to report to the Maccabean leader.

Now firmly ensconced on the plateau, Bacchides declined to move on Jerusalem and began a series of manoeuvres designed to gain control of the area and force Judas out to battle on a 'field' that would allow the Seleucids to effectively deploy their powerful phalanx. It would seem that he achieved this in part by resorting to a deliberate policy of terror in those territories under his army's immediate jurisdiction.

Bacchides was aware that there were those in the Jewish ranks who would be content to settle for less than political independence if religious freedom was assured by the Seleucids. He also knew that Judas needed to move quickly before the campaign dragged on and the people's support and willingness to fight the Seleucids began to flag. Thus, Bacchides was certain that Judas could not afford to stand by and watch as Jewish lives were wasted by his men. He was appealing both to Judas' heart and head in enticing him to battle, and the appeal was successful.

Myth of Battle

According to the account of the battle in the *First Book of Maccabees*, Judas marched to do battle with Bacchides with a force of some 3000 'picked' men. The Jewish forces established their camp at Elasa, with about a kilometre separating the two forces. The account then explains that on seeing the huge size of the enemy forces, the Jewish forces were terrified and many slipped out of camp, until no more than 800 remained.

Finding he had so few men left and 'with battle now inevitable' the

Lighter Seleucid cavalry units employed for scouting, devoid of body armour and equipped with minimal weaponry.

account explains how Judas had no choice but to fight. Furthermore, Judas' harangue to his men before the battle seems to smack of a *post factum* justification of the defeat to come, tailored with the benefit of hindsight: 'Up! let us face the enemy; we may yet have the strength to fight them.' Then comes a rejection of the demand by his men for a retreat, and an appeal by Judas not to dishonour themselves – and, if necessary, accept that the end was near.

This is all very out of keeping with what we have seen of Judas' character. Whilst certainly no coward, he had not survived for so long by courting death on the battlefield if he could depart and fight another day, as after Beth-Zechariah. There would seem little reason to suppose that he had changed. Indeed his earlier defeat of Nicanor must have made him optimistic about his ability to carry the day at Elasa.

The whole incident, dependent as it is on the acceptance of only 800 men being left, seems to have been a product of the historian seeking to justify Judas' defeat without detracting from his glory.

There would seem little reason to accept 800 troops being all that Judas could bring to battle. There is the indirect evidence that the Maccabean forces possessed heavy troops and a phalanx, and clearly Judas was able

The Seleucid cavalry who brought about the deaths of Judas and his men away from the battlefield of Elasa were probably units of the guard cavalry with whom Bacchides was serving at the time.

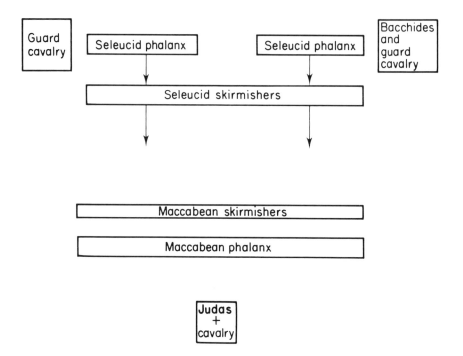

to deploy cavalry at Elasa and was himself fighting on that day from
horseback.

Similarly it is from the Biblical text's silence about the composition of
the Maccabean forces, allied to the absurd claims about its small size, that
we get an idea as to the motivation of the historian.

One final small observation concerning the Maccabean forces is in the
end the most telling. We are led to believe that, on a battlefield of their
own choosing, some of the best soldiers in the Seleucid army, including
at the most some 10,000 phalangites, took from 'morning until evening'
(1 *Maccabees* 9:13) to defeat this small force of 800 Maccabeans.

To render this battle more credible, we must assume a considerably
larger Maccabean force comprised of heavy troops forming a phalanx,
and supported by light forces with cavalry. We will also now proceed on
the assumption that Judas gave battle willingly, seeing no reason to fear
the outcome.

Reality and Tragedy

On the morning of the battle, Bacchides assembled his force in the
conventional Seleucid battle line. The heavy troops were drawn up in
two divisions, forming two phalanxes each about 4000 strong. The
cavalry were on the wings with a predominance being given to the right

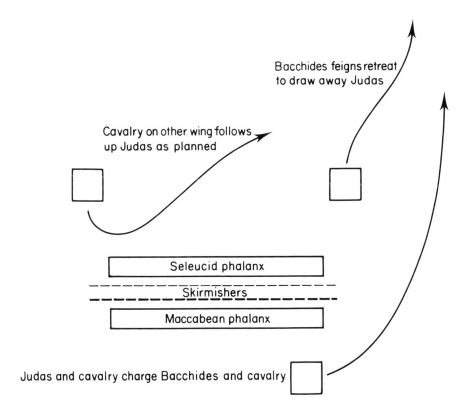

Bacchides feigns retreat
to draw away Judas

Cavalry on other wing follows
up Judas as planned

Seleucid phalanx

Skirmishers

Maccabean phalanx

Judas and cavalry charge Bacchides and cavalry

in which Bacchides himself was serving. The whole line was screened by as many as 10,000 skirmishers and it was they who closed with the Maccabean line first. Following behind the screen, the phalanx advanced in its two divisions and clashed with its Maccabean counterpart. The cavalry were held back in accordance with what seems to have been a predetermined plan to draw the Maccabean cavalry, including Judas, away from the field of battle.

At this point Judas, seeing Bacchides, launched his own cavalry at the Seleucid right wing. He was trying to repeat the tactic that had succeeded against Nicanor, whose army had disintegrated once the commander was killed. Seeing the enemy charge, the much more experienced and better trained Seleucid cavalry wheeled about and began to ride away from the field of battle, giving the impression to Judas and his men that they were retreating. After watching the Jewish cavalry follow their comrades, the left wing of the Seleucid cavalry also wheeled away from the battle line and gave full chase to Judas and his men. It was nearly 12 kilometres from the field of battle and well away from any Maccabean support that the Seleucid cavalry turned their horses and charged at Judas and his men. It was probably only then, as the left wing of the Seleucid cavalry hove into view in their rear, that Judas realised what had happened.

There was no way out. After six years of humiliating their armies and imposing on them a string of defeats, the Seleucids now had Judas Maccabeus in their grasp. Caught between two fires, the Maccabean troopers and their leader paid the enemy dear before they were speared from their horses with the long lances of the Seleucid troopers. Abandoning the bodies of Judas and his men, the Seleucid cavalry rode back to Elasa to help the phalanx defeat the remaining Maccabean forces. No doubt the Maccabean line wavered and finally broke as the Seleucid cavalry announced the death of Judas to their comrades. So fell a most remarkable man.

After the Hammer

The Bible itself records the burial of Judas and the reaction of the people he had done so much to save:

Jonathan and Simon took their brother Judas and buried him in his ancestral tomb at Modein. All Israel wept and mourned him deeply and for many days they repeated this dirge, 'what a downfall for the strong man, the man who kept Israel safe!' The other deeds of Judas, the battles he fought, the exploits he performed, and all his titles to greatness have not been recorded; but they were very many.

(1 *Maccabees* 9:19–22)

Judas Maccabeus had not lived to realise his dream of a homeland for his people, free from the political domination of the Seleucid empire. However, the mantle of striving to achieve such an end to ensure that the Jews would never again find their religious identity under threat was inherited by his brother Jonathan and, following his death, their brother Simon. It was not until 142 B.C., some eighteen years after the death of the 'Hammer' at Elasa that Simon finally forced the capitulation of the Akra in Jerusalem on the 23rd day of the Jewish month of Iyyar. Thus it was Simon, of the House of Hasmon, who made the Jews independent of the Seleucids: 'thus was the yoke of the heathen taken away from Israel'.

The grateful people of Judaea conferred upon Simon and his descendents permanent authority as the ruling High Priests of Israel.

The first foreign power to congratulate Simon and recognise him as a legitimate independent ruler and friend was the Senate of the Roman people. How ironic, therefore, that it was these same Romans who less than eighty years later brought to a close Judaea's brief independence when the clump of boots on the cobblestones of Jerusalem's streets heralded the arrival of the legions of Pompey the Great and the beginning of a domination that was to last for centuries.

Chronology of Events

301 B.C. Palestine comes under the rule of the Ptolemies of Egypt.

202 B.C. Fifth Syrian War with Seleucids under Antiochus III.

198 B.C. Palestine passes to Seleucid control; Anthiochus III confirms religious freedom of Jewish people.

190 B.C. Following disastrous attempt to invade Greece in 192 B.C., Antiochus III defeated decisively by Romans at Battle of Magnesia.

188 B.C. Treaty of Apamea; Romans force Antiochus III to give up all territories in Asia Minor west of Taurus Mountains; massive war indemnity of 15,000 talents imposed, repayable over 12 years; Antiochus III forced to send third son, Antiochus, to Rome as a hostage.

187 B.C. Antiochus III killed in Elam attempting to rob temple to help pay war indemnity; Seleucus IV succeeds to Seleucid throne.

177 B.C. Seleucus forced to send his second son Demetrius to Rome in place of Antiochus; released Antiochus makes his way to Athens.

175 B.C. Seleucus IV is assassinated; Antiochus seizes throne from usurper Heliodorus; declares himself King Antiochus IV.

174 B.C. Antiochus replaces Onias by Jason as Jewish High Priest; Jason sets out to 'Hellenize' Judaism; secures by bribery royal assent to built gymnasium in Jerusalem.

172 B.C. Jason ousted by Menelaus through payment of larger bribe to Antiochus.

169 B.C. Antiochus assumes further title Theos Epiphanes ('god manifest'); invades Egypt but forced to retreat and return to Antioch; insurrection in Jerusalem; Seleucid soldiers carry out massacre; Temple plundered with help of Menelaus.

168 B.C. Invades Egypt again; forced to retire under threat from Rome; Apollonius sent to Jerusalem to suppress further insurrection; massacres, and city walls demolished; fortress 'Akra' constructed to shelter pro-Hellenist Jews and Seleucids.

167 B.C. Antiochus orders proscription of Jewish faith; all Jewish rituals and practices forbidden on pain of death; in December orders image of Olympian Zeus erected in Temple. Harsh persecution begins.

166 B.C. Mattathias raises flag of revolt; takes to hills with sons to fight guerrilla war against Seleucids and apostate Jews; Hasidim join the rebels; Mattathias succeeded by third son Judas; Judas defeats Seleucid forces of Apollonius; Seron's force defeated at Beth-Horon.

165 B.C. Judas defeats large Seleucid army at Emmaus.

164 B.C. Lysias defeated by Judas at Beth-Zur; returns to Jerusalem rededicating Temple; Antiochus IV dies campaigning against Parthians.

163 B.C. Judas campaigns in territories surrounding Judaea to liberate Jews under persecution from Seleucid supporters; unsuccessful attempt to take Akra by siege; Lysias and boy king Antiochus V invade Judaea; major battle at Beth-Zechariah; the Maccabean army vanquished; Seleucid siege of Jerusalem abandoned after attempted coup in Antioch forces Lysias to return; decree of 167 B.C. repealed; religious freedom guaranteed; city walls destroyed; Menelaus executed.

162 B.C. Demetrius returns from Rome; kills Lysias and Antiochus V; becomes Demetrius I; Alcimus made High Priest.

161 B.C. Alcimus returns to Jerusalem with soldiers under Bacchides; killing of 60 Hasidim causes new rebellion; Judas defeats and kills Nicanor at Adasa; concludes treaty of 'Friendship and Alliance' with the Romans.

160 B.C. Demetrius despatches army to Judaea under Bacchides; Judas Maccabeus killed at Battle of Elasa.

Bibliography

Anderson, B. *The Living World of the Old Testament* Longman, 1976.

Bar-Kochva, B. *The Seleucid Army* Cambridge University Press, 1976.

Bright, J. *A History of Israel*, 3rd Edition, Philadelphia, 1981.

Ferrill, A. *The Origins of War* Thames and Hudson, 1986.

Filson, F.V. *A New Testament History* SCM, 1964.

Grant, M. *The History of Ancient Israel*, Weidenfeld & Nicolson, 1984.

Grant, M. *The Ancient Mediterranean* Weidenfeld & Nicolson, 1969.

Head, D. *Armies of the Macedonian and Punic Wars*, Wargames Research Group, 1982.

Humble, R. *Warfare in the Ancient World* Cassell BCA, 1980.

Jagersma, J. *A History of Israel from Alexander the Great to Bar-Kochva* SCM, 1985.

Noth, M.A. *History of Israel* SCM, 1958.

Pfeiffer, R. *History of New Testament Times* A. & C. Black, 1963.

Pritchard, J. (ed) *The Times Atlas of the Bible* Times Books, 1987.

Russell, D.S. *The Meaning and Message of Jewish Apocalyptic* SCM, 1964.

Index

Page numbers in *italics* refer to illustrations.

Illustrations
Colour plates by Richard Hook
Line illustrations by Suzie Hole and Chesca Potter
Maps and diagrams by Chartwell Illustrators
Photographs and other illustrations courtesy of: BIPAC (page 83); Directorate of Antiquities and Heritage, Baghdad (pages 105, 113, 127 and 130); Iraqi Cultural Centre, London (pages 135, 139 and 140); Jewish Education Bureau (page 173); Kobal Collection (page 77); Trustees of the British Museum (pages 13, 14, 16, 17, 21, 22, 35, 56, 61, 69, 75, 79, 125, 133, 146, 147, 148, 149 and 179); Zev Radovan, Jerusalem (pages 25, 27, 31, 35, 37, 153, 161, 163, 170, 171 and 179); Voderasiatisches Museum, Berlin (page 131).

192